MY PATH TO THE DUNDAS VALLEY

by

The Honourable Thomas A. Beckett, Q.C.

Edited by Meralee Beckett and Mary-Jo Land

2018

Dedicated to my family
and all other lovers of nature.

Cartoon by Blaine

Our task must be to free ourselves by widening our circle of compassion to embrace all living creatures and the whole of nature and its beauty.

Albert Einstein
1879-1955

Forward

Being in a crowded cafe with Tom Beckett in Dundas, Ontario, for that is where he has lived for many years, is a theatrical moment. This man is speaking to everyone. He winds up like an old-fashioned record player and, with the rich voice of the judge, lawyer and politician that he was, begins a story. It seems as though everyone within earshot is listening. And he listens carefully to you, because he does not steal the stage. And he is magnetic in the telling.

This is Tom Beckett, one of Canada's first and most effective environmentalists. It is the man to whom countless numbers of us owe the saving of the Dundas Valley from yet another development or highway. Not to mention the enormous success of the Hamilton Conservation Authority which saw fit to name a forest Thomas A. Beckett because he led the fights and won political backing, raised millions of dollars and had the creative vision to see what had to be done.

Beckett was an "activist" without knowing the word. He just got on with it. And that is where all the stories come in. For Beckett has a basketful of them, starting with an accomplished family — more stories — and even mysteries, political dirty fighting, attempts at bribery and even murder.

And some of the tales will arouse our own memories, because of the names and events mostly forgotten. He brings backroom shenanigans to life with his stories and a light brush. Yet there is about his stories no self-admiration, although a story he tells about his adventure with the Ku Klux Klan in the US is an insight into his determination to follow his own instincts.

For a man who's done so much for his country, proper recognition has been slow in coming. But the stories speak for themselves.

Gordon Bullock,

Publisher Emeritus, Hamilton Spectator

June 2018

Introduction

Here I am, 92 years old and writing a book. It sounds like a bit of madness but I am assured by those around me that senility has not quite caught up with me yet.

A few years ago, I met a charming Hamilton doctor named Bill Bensen, who sadly, is no longer with us. He told me that he and his friends were frequent hikers in the Dundas Valley. He was aware of my early connections with the Conservation Authority and thought that its history should be written. He insisted I should do it and in a moment of weakness, I assured him I would do just that. I am not sure that a guy my age should have undertaken such a project, especially as my two main character traits are laziness and procrastination. These two things plus my inability to type and my limited vision are all that stood in my way. But maybe better late than never, as they say.

When I started out, the book was intended to be about the early days of the Authority, but it soon morphed into more of an autobiography and has ended up being a little of both. It is intended as a work of non-fiction, but with my failing memory and natural biases, it may, although unintentionally, slip from time to time into the other category. I think that those who do this for a living call it "literary license".

I could not have written this book without the assistance of a number of people. With respect to the Spencer Creek and Hamilton Conservation Authorities, I received a lot of help from Wayne Terryberry, who is the Outdoor Recreation and Natural Land Coordinator at McMaster University. Wayne has supplied me with various documents, particularly his MA thesis on the creation of the Spencer Creek Conservation Authority, which he completed in 2016.

I am indebted to my granddaughter Angelica Land, who upon graduating from Carleton University in the spring of 2017, spent several weeks with me as my eyes and hands. I am also grateful to my son-in-law Kevin Land, who is a playwright and author, for his valued assistance and input. But I am particularly indebted to my daughter Mary-Jo Land and to my wife Meralee who both spent countless hours as my advisors and editors during the development of this book.

Tom

September 1 2018

Part 1

The Early Years

Early Influences

I remember the first time I saw the Dundas Valley. It was September, 1945. I was 19 years old and taking my first train trip from Windsor to Toronto to start my University days. The train stopped at the little station in Dundas at what we now know as Spencer Gorge. I remember looking over that valley and thinking how wonderful to have such a huge wilderness area situated right beside the city of Hamilton. I could not have dreamed that that scene would play such a huge role in my life.

I have often been asked how I became involved in conservation and why it became such a passion in my life. The answer is I don't really know, but I do know that every experience, large or small, good or bad, and nearly every person we meet and book we read, plays some role in shaping our character and values. Maybe genetics plays a role too, not just in the way we look but to some extent in the way we think. The age-old question again, how much is nature and how much is nurture.

To the extent that I have a sense of humour (and I think I have a pretty good one) I credit my mother, Josephine, or Joe as she was known, who was loving and caring and one of the funniest persons I ever knew. My father, Harold C. Beckett, was born and raised in Hamilton, the son of a well-to-do businessman. I think my love of open spaces, trees, water and wildlife started with the genes I inherited from him. I know that as a very young man, before World War I, he was a frequent visitor to Algonquin Park and often took canoe trips through its near-deserted lakes. I am intrigued by the thought that somewhere while sweating his way over a portage, he might have bumped into Tom Thomson under his grey canoe heading in the opposite direction. Perhaps they would have stopped and chatted. My Dad talked to every soul he met. Maybe, they would have talked about painting as my father was also a painter.

My family has had long connections with the Park. My grandfather Henry Charles Beckett had a cottage on Cache Lake for his family of one girl and six boys. Later, one of my father's brothers had a cottage on Canoe Lake and another owned one on Smoke Lake. My cousins still have the Smoke Lake cottage. My first connection with the Park was as a counsellor at Taylor Statten Camp on Canoe Lake. It was there that I met the woman that I was to marry three years later, Joan Baden-Powell.

My canoe trips in Algonquin are embedded in my memory forever. I even met the ghost of Tom Thomson one night out canoeing on the Lake. More about that encounter later. However, between meeting Tom Thomson's ghost, falling in love and having one of the best times of my life that summer, how could the emotions and memories of Canoe Lake and Algonquin Park not have been deeply etched in the innermost depths of my being?

I also have wonderful memories of the Rocky Mountains where I was a tour bus driver for Jasper Park Lodge in the summer of '48. For that entire summer, day after day, I was able to drive those breath-taking roads in and around Jasper and Banff and experience those majestic mountains. Those scenes, experiences and memories contributed to the person I became, one with a near obsession for saving trees and valleys. They presented a new array of sights and sounds and encounters with wildlife. I guess I became what some others called, with a touch of derision and sarcasm at the time, a "Tree Hugger". To this day, I have not really understood why being a person who cares about trees is such a bad thing.

I tell you these things because I am sure my love of beauty and open spaces was cultivated by all those experiences. The feeling I get when I walk along a forest trail or look at a waning sunset on a quiet lake is something that has been with me for as long as I can recall. Perhaps that is why my anger is aroused whenever I see a natural area overrun by development.

There was nothing I learned at Law School that could account for my love of natural places but no doubt my time in Law sparked another talent or affliction, depending how you look at it. I have always been a bit of a rabble rouser and fighter for what I see as just causes, whether for free speech in Assumption College in Windsor, or my opposition to the Vietnam war or the destruction of a beautiful valley by a four-lane highway. These characteristics have been the driving force all my life. I have learned that even in the face of criticism and opposition, the important thing was to fight for what you believe in, no matter how loud and hurtful the voices of opposition are. In the end, whether you win or lose, you have the satisfaction of knowing that you did the right thing and fought for the honourable and just side of the issue.

Family History

Before I tell you about my early days growing up in Windsor, I should tell you something about my ancestral roots in Hamilton, which as it turned out, played an important role in how I came to spend much of my life in that city as an adult.

My ancestors on both the sides of my family are of English descent. My great grandfather, Charles Beckett, was born in Cheshire in 1834 and subsequently emigrated to Hamilton. He was a professor of music and the organist at Christ Church Cathedral. My great grandmother, Harriet Gillard, was born in Devon. She also emigrated to Hamilton and married my great-grandfather in May, 1858. My grandfather, Henry Charles Beckett was born in Hamilton in 1860. He married Edith Champ in 1886. They had seven children, one girl, and then six boys, the eldest of whom was my father, Harold.

Edith Champ Beckett and Henry Charles Beckett

Those of you familiar with Beckett Drive, a major and very beautiful mountain access road in the west end of the city, might be interested to know that this road was built as a toll road by Frederick Garner Beckett who was the brother of my great-grandfather Charles. He was a manufacturer and major land owner on the mountain. He put the toll booth at the bottom of the road in order to pay for construction costs. Some years later he dedicated the road to the city and it became known as Beckett Drive. I am very pleased that one of the loveliest roads in Hamilton bears my family name.

My grandfather Henry was a well-respected and well-loved man. They say his funeral procession in 1922 was one of the largest ever in Hamilton up until then. He headed a large wholesale grocery business, W. H. Gillard and Company. He certainly seemed creative and imaginative. Back when airplanes were beginning to appear as novelties, he hired one to fly over Hamilton and dump bags of tiny red-dyed feathers over the city. As they fluttered down, people were mystified and curious as to what this meant. The next day, the Hamilton Spectator carried large ads announcing the introduction of Red Feather Spices, a new brand for my grandfather's company. Red Feather was a well-known brand in Canada for many years.

My grandfather also owned Imperial Vinegar, which later became Canada Vinegar. He built and owned the roller rink on James Street and was one of the investors in the Royal Connaught Hotel. Interestingly, one of his partners in this venture was Bill Southam and many years later, I leased space in the same hotel, including Southam's office in the penthouse, for my law office.

My grandfather did not always succeed in business. Long before WW1, he, along with four other men, each invested fifty-thousand dollars in a goldmine at Saw Bill Lake in Northern Ontario. The mine failed and my grandfather lost his money. However, he had picked up a gold nugget at the site and had it made into a ring which he gave to my father years later, who in turn gave it to me when I was 14 years old. It has been on my finger ever since, nearly eight decades later.

In 1903, my grandparents moved to a lovely Victorian home at 114 Charlton Street West. My grandmother led a leisurely life of a proper Edwardian lady in the city. She owned the first electric car in Hamilton, bought to carry her and lady friends, who did not want to get soiled, to afternoon bridge and tea parties. Unfortunately, I never met my grandfather as he died before I was born and I have only a vague recollection of my grandmother Edith.

The Beckett family certainly had an affinity with the outdoors. They acquired a site on Cache Lake in Algonquin Park in the earliest days after it was made into a provincial park. It was less cottage, more campground. There, the family gathered to do what they appeared to love best, and that was to spend their time in canoes. My father, being the oldest boy, often took one or more of his younger brothers on canoe trips in the park. From time to time, when no one else was available, my father went tripping with a guide or by himself. I remember him telling me about camping on Big Trout Lake, one of the most beautiful lakes in the park. One evening, he spotted a campfire across the lake and paddled over to join two Americans who were camping there. One of them had something in his hand he called a zipper, a new invention he said. My Dad thought it didn't have much chance of replacing the button.

    Algonquin Park seems part of our fabric. My Uncle KC had a cottage on Canoe Lake, near the Portage Store, for many years. My Uncle Reg built a cottage on Smoke Lake in the early 50s and it is still being enjoyed by the Elyria, Ohio, Becketts to this day. My uncles would be pleased to know that I was made an Honorary Life Member of the Algonquin Wildlands League, a result of my advocacy to preserve both Algonquin and Quetico Provincial Parks from excessive logging.

    My father was a remarkable man. His interest in architecture must have started well before he entered University. I remember him telling me about working for a time for a Hamilton architect by the name of Arthur Peane at the corner of King and James. My father worked on the drawings for a theatre in Dundas, now a health food store called the Horn of Plenty. He then went on to Columbia University in New York City to study architecture where he graduated, in 1915, with five Ecole de Beaux Artes medals.

In 1917, he enlisted in the Army as a commissioned officer. I assume he was made an officer because he was a university graduate. He served with the 124th Battalion. However, before he was sent to France he became very ill with some respiratory ailment and was eventually mustered out of the Army. Good thing, likely. His younger brother Gerald served in France in 1915 and 1916 in the frontline trenches. He came home physically injured from gas attacks and psychologically affected with "shell shock". His father arranged a brass band at the train station in Hamilton for his homecoming. Uncle Reg, who served on the front lines from 1917 to the end of the war luckily came home unscathed.

Subsequently, in 1918, my father moved to Detroit, which, in those days, was a very fine city. That year, he met and married my mother, Josephine Toull, on the 18th of October. There was a bit of a depression following the war, but for a short time my father earned a good living as a commercial artist. This was before the days when photography took over in advertising. About this time, he was offered a job in Hollywood as a set designer but he turned it down because he didn't think movies had much of a future. I can only speculate as to what my life would have been like had we moved to Hollywood!

My father's career in architecture finally took off in the early 20s. He became one of Michigan's most outstanding architects and was the choice of many of the motor kings of Detroit. By the latter half of the decade, he was designing and building many of the finest homes in Michigan. One of the homes was the Harper House in Lansing. Mr. Harper owned a company which manufactured most of the wheels for the auto industry at that time. The Harper House won second prize for the most beautiful house built in Michigan in 1929. First prize that year went to the Edsel Ford home in Grosse Point; however, it cost ten times as much to build. The gardens at the Harper House, which my father also designed and built, did win first prize that year.

The gardens consisted mainly of a large reflecting pool surrounded by exotic stone works that my father imported from a site near Peterborough, Ontario. He had been fishing in the area and had come across a dry riverbed filled with beautiful and unique looking rock that had been etched over the eons by flowing water. Recognizing their value, he had a rail spur built to the site and had the rock hauled to the Harper House. R. E. Olds, the owner of Oldsmobile, was a neighbour and when he saw the stone, insisted on a load for his property as well. It is interesting to note that Olds also used the Harper House as the backdrop in many of the advertisements of his latest Oldsmobiles.

My father was by any measure in those latter years of the 1920s, a very successful young man.

Jefferson Boulevard

In 1925, my father and mother, then living in Detroit, bought some property on Jefferson Boulevard, in Riverside, Ontario, which is now part of Windsor. My father built a house there just prior to my birth, as a temporary home pending the construction of a large Tudor style home on the corner of Jefferson Blvd. and Riverside Drive. I was born in the master bedroom of the house on December the 23rd, 1925. My older brother Bill, had been born in Detroit in 1920, while my younger brother, John, was also born in the Jefferson house in 1928.

37 Jefferson Blvd. Windsor Ontario

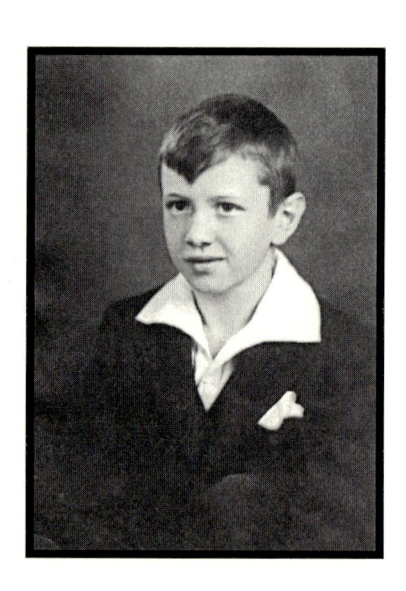

Tom, age 10 years

Jefferson Boulevard was a wonderful place for a kid to grow up. It had about a dozen houses on each side. It was a wide boulevard lined with stately American Elms and I remember them as rather enormous. Sadly, they all fell victim to Dutch Elm Disease in the 60s and 70s. Jefferson was a great playground for us kids. And to make it even more fun, the people on our street collectively owned a piece of riverfront property on the Detroit River at the foot of Jefferson, which had a private bathing beach and a swimming raft. A good deal of our lives as young kids was spent at that beach swimming and just hanging out. The father of my pal Bunny owned a small motor boat which provided us with many days of adventure on the River and on Lake St Clair.

We used to visit Peach Island a lot. It was an island of about 100 acres, located where Lake St. Clair empties into the Detroit River, and crisscrossed by old canals dug many years before for a development that never happened. The canals were overgrown with trees and vines; we always felt like we were adventuring into mystical places and treacherous terrain.

My mother was always terrified of water, as she could not swim, and she imposed very strict rules on us about going down to the river to swim unless someone was there to watch us. In point of fact, she was probably right to be concerned since the river had a fairly swift current once you were out some distance from shore.

During the winter, the river became a place to skate and play hockey. It would freeze from the shoreline out to where it was flowing at a fairly fast rate and except for a very few winters it never froze over between our side and the Belle Isle side in Detroit. I remember that when we played hockey and needed a drink of water we would go out to the edge of the ice where the river was flowing swiftly and get down on our stomachs to get a drink. In hindsight, quite dangerous! A friend of mine, Bill Flanders, was doing that once when a section of the ice he was on suddenly broke free and started sailing down the river. Fortunately, the floe was big enough that he had a fairly safe craft for his journey. He was finally spotted and rescued when he reached the Windsor area, about four miles downstream.

On another occasion, I went skating by myself. I'm sure my mother did not know about this. I remember skating upstream on the river on good ice but after going some distance I noticed the ice ahead looked very thin. I got it into my head that if I skated fast enough over the ice I wouldn't break through. I got an early lesson in physics and immediately went through the ice about a hundred feet out from the end of the nearest dock. It was an extremely cold and sunny day and no one else was around. Those were the days before lightweight warm clothing and I was dressed in a heavy woollen outfit. I knew I would drown unless I made it to the end of the nearby dock where I could climb out of the water. As you guessed, I did not drown: I made it out of the water and being the rather shy child that I was, I did not go to the nearest house for help. Instead I plodded home, a good half mile or more away, in my skates and sopping wet clothes which quickly turned to solid ice. When I got home the maid had to help me out of all my stuff. Needless to say, it was an incident I made sure my mother never learned of, for obvious reasons.

Nobody on our street ever seemed to move. I don't think the depression hit them to the same extent as it did many others. It was a street of professionals and motor executives, all of whom remained employed, except for my father who did not earn a nickel from 1930 until 1935. He kept his office open for a year after the Crash as he did not want to put his staff out of work. Being unemployed for my dad must have been very, very tough as he was a real workaholic. He kept busy gardening and painting. He painted in watercolours and the beautiful flowers he grew were his favourite subjects. If my dad didn't have a nervous breakdown during that time, he certainly deserved one.

I remember growing up witnessing a great deal of worry. Constant worry. And yet to others who suffered real poverty in the Depression we hardly seemed to be suffering. We continued to have help in the house. They were part of my life: Elsa, Irene, Gladys and others. We had them not because we had money but because my mother was a serious asthmatic and could do nothing strenuous. Even brushing her own hair would bring on an attack. It seems my father had managed to set aside something from the good days to sustain us into the Thirties.

On the Road

In the spring of 1932, with nothing much else to do, my parents decided to rent the house for a year, pile the family and Laddie, our collie, into the family car and take off. We had a very luxurious 1929 Buick Sedan, painted two tones of green with dark green velvet upholstery, wooden spoke wheels and spare tires set in the front wheel wells. The car was a leftover from the good days.

So, in late April we set out and headed north. Again, I have no direct recollection of this journey but I can tell you that we got to a place near Calendar, Ontario and set up our camp for the summer at Joe's Fishing Camp on Lake Nosbonsing. My dad told Joe Gauthier, the owner, that he needed a better name and suggested Big Moose Camp, a name which it carries to this day. As a favour to Joe, my Dad painted a large beautiful sign depicting a majestic bull moose in its natural habitat which was placed out on highway 11, just south of Calendar. There was an immediate influx of tourists to the camp, so many that Joe was not able to accommodate them all.

By September, we had had enough of fishing and I am sure my mother had had enough of Big Moose Camp. We moved on, largely over unpaved roads, through Ottawa, into Quebec and then on to the new highway around the shore of the Gaspe Peninsula. I am told that after the official party cut the ribbon, we were the first car over the line to travel the new road. We spent some weeks there, at Cap Chat, boarding with a French-Canadian family, and then meandered slowly down the east coast of the United States until we reached the little town of Fort Lauderdale. It was barely more than one main street and the coastal highway, the A1A, which ran through, still unpaved. Miraculously, my mother's asthma disappeared immediately once we got there so we took an apartment just off the beach and stayed the winter from November until April.

We spent every day at the beach. My father used to do marathon swims along the shore out beyond the breakers and my mother, my brothers and I would follow him along on the beach. One day, two good-sized sharks tried to attack him; one coming up beneath him and actually lifting him out of the water. My dad made a beeline to the shore and from that day forward he restricted his swimming to the beach in Fort Lauderdale which was supervised by lifeguards.

I remember there was a lot of Portuguese man o'war along the beach. They were like large blue bubbles with many thread-like tentacles averaging thirty feet long trailing behind them as the wind propelled them across the water. As kids, we learned to swim in front of them but once in a while an unknowing tourist would make the mistake of getting entangled in the tentacles and suffer agonizing stings. I remember the lifeguards treating their stings with ammonia.

Anyway, at age six it was a great winter for me.

My Illness

Sometime after we got home that spring, something happened to me, that without a doubt, altered the course of my life.

I was swinging in a tree in the orchard behind our house when I suddenly became very ill. I was alone but reached the house before passing out. Without going into great detail, I can tell you the doctors were called, including a specialist who decided I was too ill to be transported to the hospital by ambulance.

He said that to move me was likely to kill me. They had concluded that my heart had dilated to fill my entire chest as a result of an earlier overdose of digitalis that had been improperly administered for an illness, which, as it turned out, I did not have in the first place.

I remember the doctor had an orange Parker fountain pen which he used to mark the outline of my heart on my chest. I was supposed to only lie on my back and if I did turn, it was only to be on the right side and only with assistance. The trouble was I did not feel the slightest bit ill and unbeknownst to everyone I would often get out of bed and sit looking out the window at the other kids playing in the street. My mother once caught me doing this. She was a bit horrified at what I was doing and I felt very guilty. Later in my life, I learned from heart specialists that my diagnosis was undoubtedly wrong. Anyway, for the next five years, I was treated more or less like an invalid; with no strenuous activity like tennis or other athletic endeavours.

One reason it changed the course of my life, is that when I tried to enlist in the RCAF in 1943 and in the Army in 1944, I was rejected as medically unfit because of this history. It seems a bit silly now but in the naivety of youth, there was nothing I wanted to do more than go to war. More about that later.

Better Times

In 1935, after five years of being idle, good fortune came to my father. Prime Minister R. B. Bennett knew of the exquisite homes and gardens that Hamiltonian HC Beckett had built in Michigan and Windsor. Bennett appointed my father Dominion Government Architect, to design and build the new Administration Building in Banff. That building, as well as the Park Gate building and the Cascade Gardens, which he also designed and built, are now world famous. I was told by the Superintendent of the Gardens that everyone who works there must learn who Harold Beckett was. To this day, they follow his planting schemes meticulously. During the year and a half or so of construction, my father was a very important man in Banff. One year, he led the annual Indian Days parade on horseback.

In 1936, when the Government changed from Bennett to Mackenzie King, the Banff project came to a halt before all the projects my father had planned were completed. From there, he went to Purdue University as Director of Housing Research for the Rockefeller Foundation. While my father was at Purdue, the rest of the family spent the winter of 1937 in Delray Beach, Florida. It was there that I met Ann Goodspeed, who lived with her family across the street from us and that winter and when we were eleven, she became my first girlfriend. I never forgot her and many years later through the magic of the Internet we made contact and remain in close touch.

In the summers of 1937 and 1938, I went to Camp Kitchekwana on Beausoleil Island near Honey Harbour in Georgian Bay. There, I earned my Royal Life Saving medals which enabled me to take a job some years later as a life guard. It was there I also learned to sail but most importantly, it was where I learned the wonders of the canoe and went on my first canoe trip. I remember crossing Go Home Bay in white-water conditions and dumping our canoe in the rapids on the Moon River. Canoe trips for young boys of this age stay with you all your life.

John, Tom and Bill with Josephine (Joe)

Ann Goodspeed, and Tom, Del Ray Beach FL, 1937

Assumption College

The Dirty Thirties finally came to a halt and were replaced with the next world calamity on September 3 1939, when WW2 broke out. Sometime around then, my father reopened his architectural office in Detroit as things had begun to look up. I started high school in September 1940. Normally, I would have gone to Walkerville Collegiate Institute in Windsor. But for reasons that never seemed convincing to me, my mother decided I should go to Assumption College, a Catholic boys-only high school operated by the Basilian Order. While we were not Catholic, she thought the influence of all those fine priests would be good for me. Later on, I think I discerned my mother's real motive, which was to keep me away from all those pretty girls that I would have met at Walkerville.

I soon learned at Assumption that, as with any group of men, some were good and others were not. I saw far too much violence committed by priests against students, which was prevalent at the time. Eventually, I acquired an element of immunity from this following an incident in which I had my head cut open after a priest-in-training fired a blackboard eraser at me when I was speaking to a student behind me, between classes. I did not want my mother to find out but unfortunately the maid, Irene, told her. As I would have predicted, she stormed off to see the Principal, Father Thompson, warning him that her son was not to be hit any place except in accord with prescribed methods, which I think meant the strap on the hands.

Tom, age 14

Tom, age 14

Like I said, I was a good student at Assumption College. However, I found the authoritarianism of the Basilians hard to take. On three or four occasions, I found myself in deep conflict with one or two of the priests. It was never a matter of misbehaviour but rather some standoff on some issue or principle for me. Anyway, when I went to register for my fourth year, Father Thompson said he thought I should go to another school. Interestingly, about seven years later, after graduating from University, I bumped into that same principal, Father Thompson, on a back street in Calgary. After a nice chat and as we were parting, he said to me, "I was Principal of Assumption College for fifteen years and never during that time did I have a student I respected more than you." I don't think anyone has ever said anything to me that had more impact on my life.

I tell you this story because as it turns out Assumption did have a very positive influence on me, but perhaps not in the way my mother had intended. It was because of that comment made some seven years later, on that street in Calgary.

The War Years

On December 7th 1941, the Japanese Imperial Fleet attacked Pearl Harbour and on Monday, December 8th, the United States froze all shipments of steel. On December 10th, my father closed his office for the second time in a decade and went to work for The United States Department of Ordinance with the nominal rank of Major. He went to Des Moines, Iowa and in three months designed and built, in a corn field, a factory turning out 50,000 50-calibre machine gun bullets a day. It was a very interesting building. The entire wall of the assembly line was a waterfall, the purpose of which was to eliminate static electricity which could be dangerous in a building containing highly volatile explosives. Surrounding the plant at the end of rubber walkways, like the spokes of a wheel, were concrete pill boxes where fulminate of mercury was stored, a very unstable explosive that went into the manufacture of the cartridges on the assembly line.

After the plant was completed, he went on to work on the design of US military vehicles in what was known as the Tank Office in downtown Detroit. I remember him telling me he was asked to design the snorkel that would be fitted on tanks to allow them to operate while almost fully submerged. This was because many of the South Pacific Islands they would have to retake were surrounded by reefs and lagoons through which the tanks had to cross. The design was completed in only forty-eight hours after which it went into production. My dad had transformed himself from an architect of fine homes into a mechanical engineer!

I may have told you what an amazing man my dad was; kind, loving, forgiving and tolerant. He did not practice any brand of religion or politics. He would smoke pipes and cigarettes but never inhaled. He loved his scotch but I never saw him drink to excess. He never laid a hand on us or anybody else. His sense of humour was underdeveloped: he wanted to be funny and loved humour but never quite learned how to tell a good joke. My father was about the best natured person I have ever known.

Our family used to play terrible practical jokes on him. For example, we always heard him get up in the morning and moan and groan as though he hadn't slept a wink. So, one night we decided to advance the clocks in the house, including the alarm clock, and set it to go off about hour after he went to bed. In the meantime, we had turned out all the lights and gone to bed ourselves. We heard him get up, moan and groan, shave, and then go downstairs to make his lunch. He left the house in total darkness and walked up the street to catch the streetcar. At this point, I could not stand it any longer and I ran after him. "Dad, it's only a joke!" I said, "It's only 10:30!". The poor man took it in good humour and returned to the house to go back to bed and try and get a night's sleep. What a mean trick that was!

On another occasion, my younger brother John came in one night around 11 o'clock. While he was walking beside the house after parking the car, my mother dumped a glass of water on him from her bedroom window. She knew there would be retribution so she ran and hid in bed with my father where he slept in a separate bedroom because of his snoring. She heard John come up the stairs and apparently he concluded she was in with my dad, came in, threw back the covers and poured a glass of ice-cold water on my mother and my sleeping father. Surprisingly, after the initial shock, my father took it in good stride.

My mother had a wonderful sense of humour and there was a lot of fun in our house all the years I lived there. She was also the family worrier. She was a very tender and kind-hearted woman. All my friends loved her, calling her "Mert" and we all hung out a lot at my house. During the depression years, I often saw strange men sitting at our breakfast room table. They would knock on our door asking for something to eat and Mom never turned anyone away.

Tom's Mother, Josephine Toull

Joe and Harold (circa 1962)

Fowl Days

During the war a lot of commodities like gasoline, meat, butter and eggs were rationed. You were given ration coupons and when the coupons ran out, you were out of luck. My mother, clever as she was in those times, found a way to make butter. We would go to the market and buy cream and make our own. Because meat was scarce, my father thought it would be a good idea if we acquired a few chickens and housed them in the double garage behind the house. The few chickens seem to grow: we not only had egg-laying chickens but we also bought cartons of little chicks which we then raised.

Over time, the number of birds in our garage multiplied. Some geese were added to the mix and they enjoyed our pond in the backyard as well as eating everything they could reach. Then, someone gave me a pair of racing pigeons. I never raced the pigeons but we built a loft for them in the garage. Their descendants, by the way, still live there. I also acquired a pet crow. Furthermore, for some reason my father decided to raise golden pheasants and a special pen was made for them behind the garage. In addition to all these birds we had our cocker spaniel Skippy, and a cat! It was quite a menagerie. As the war came to an end, so did the birds. It seems like my father never did things in moderation.

Tom (1943)

I Become a Deckhand

In the summer of 1942, I managed to get a job as a deckhand on the *Bayton*, a Patterson Steamship Lines bulk carrier lake freighter, owned by the uncle of my lifelong friend Dick Larkin, who also worked on the *Bayton* that summer. The *Bayton* was not all that large as lake freighters go, only 416 feet long, but it was there I had my first contact with the real world. It was an incredibly dangerous work environment and I learned a lot, especially from the older professional seamen. It was there, also, that I took note of the much better working conditions on the unionized American ships.

As I boarded the ship for the first time, in the wee hours of the night, I noticed that some of the crew members were sleeping on the deck because it was too hot in the cabins below. As we departed the docks, the captain, whose name was Glass, made a U-turn in the middle of the Detroit River right in front of an American laker coming up-river, a maneuver which led to a hail of profanities between the two captains over the loud speakers. Our ship's whistle gave five blasts, indicating immediate danger. What a way to begin my life as a seaman!

Working as a deckhand was an extremely dangerous job, especially with my inexperience. One day, the first mate asked me to paint the foremast, and even though I was terrified of heights, as a 16-

year-old boy, I did what I was told without question. To get to the top of the mast, I had to climb up a wire rope ladder. It started at the gunnels and went almost to the top of the mast. As it ascended, the ladder got narrower so that I could no longer put two feet in the wire rung, as there was only room for one. My left arm was looped around the mast holding the paint can so that my right arm was free for painting. It seemed like a calm day on Lake Superior but I guess there was a low swell on the lake. That meant that at the top of the mast, the swell was amplified, and the mast swayed back and forth above the deck, which seemed so far below. The first mate was watching me, and shouted up, "Don't you like it up there?" "No, sir." I replied. He called back up, "Come down immediately." I was so happy to do so. He said, "Don't do that again. Don't be afraid of telling people you're afraid of heights. I'm surprised you didn't end up dead on the deck."

On another occasion, we were unloading coal on Manitoulin Island. The coal was unloaded using a large bucket, suspended from a crane on the dock, which was lowered into the hold to scoop up buckets of coal. As the level of coal went down, a bulldozer was lowered into the hold to push the remaining coal into large mounds. The crew was then sent down into the hold to assist in the cleanup. As you can imagine, the noise level the crew was exposed to was horrendous. As I was starting to climb up a ladder on the bulkhead, a shipmate suddenly shoved me aside just as the bucket swung and hit the ladder near me, tearing off one of the steel rungs. I had been one second from certain death!

During that period, we had watched the Movietone News in the movie theatre and I remember the Battle of Britain and the relentless bombing of its cities. It showed cities such as London surrounded by barrage balloons, which were large blimps with steel wires hanging below them so that if an enemy warplane flew beneath them, they would have their wings sliced off. I had never actually seen barrage balloons except in the newsreels, until my ship arrived in the locks at Sault Saint Marie. As our ship approached, I noticed, to my surprise, there were many barrage balloons in the air. It was clear that no German plane could reach the locks from Germany, but if they got their hands on a plane near the area and sunk an ore-laden ship while it was in the locks, it would have had a huge negative impact on the war production in the United States. This was because most of the iron ore used in steel-making for the war effort came from the Mesabi Range in Northern Minnesota and was shipped to Superior, Wisconsin and then brought through the locks to the steels mills in Ohio and other places nearby.

Unfortunately, my summer job as a seaman didn't last long. I managed to get injured on the ship when

I accidentally dropped a hatch cover on my hand and had to spend the rest of the summer on Workman's Compensation.

I Enlist

When I turned 18 years old in December 1943, I went downtown with the intention of joining the RCAF. At that time, many of my friends and I wanted nothing more than to join the Air Force and maybe fly a Spitfire. But after going through the induction process, including the medical, I was turned down because of my heart history. It had raised its ugly head again.

However, one day about six months later I was back downtown buying some clothes when I noticed an Army recruiting station on the main street. I went in and signed up. When I asked him when I should be reporting for duty he said, "You're in now!" He said he would drive me out to my home to pick up my things and say goodbye to my mother. We pulled up in front of the house in an armoured car and I went and told my mother I had joined the Army. I don't remember my mother's reaction but I am sure it was one of shock and horror.

Then I was sent by train to an army base in London, Ontario, where I went through the induction process again. I was fairly certain I would get in this time. There was another chap going through the line just ahead of me who was wearing very thick glasses and I didn't think he would make it. As it turned out, however, he was in and I was out, again because of my heart history as a kid. Sadly, he was killed in action barely two months later.

I thought at the time I could drive an ambulance or something like that but they said that there had been heavy casualties at Caen and all they wanted was infantry. They gave me a little 'applicant-for-enlistment' button that I could wear in my lapel to show that I had attempted to enlist but I was always embarrassed to be a healthy looking young man who was not in uniform. Some people would say I was very fortunate not to have been accepted by the army, and as logical as that may seem, I have never gotten over a feeling of regret that I was not there for one of the most momentous events in the history of mankind.

Walkerville Collegiate

After Father Thompson had suggested I attend a different school, I transferred to Walkerville Collegiate Institute for Grade 12. My time at Walkerville was happy and I had a girlfriend named Barbara, who was a classical pianist. It was at Walkerville that I experienced another of my life altering events. Remember, I had gone through a period of five years when I was not supposed to partake in any strenuous activity. But the fact was I liked to run and did so at every opportunity. I did a little track training at Assumption but never to the point where I ran in a race.

In the spring, I decided to enter the Spring Track Meet. I didn't own any spiked track shoes and the track was cinder so I was clearly at a disadvantage compared to the other runners. I entered the 100, the 220, and the 440-yard races as well as the hop skip and jump and the running broad jump. I did not belong to the school's track team and I had never competed in any of these events.

One of the contestants was a senior by the name of Gordie Bell who had a reputation as Windsor's fastest sprinter. I knew little about the various sprints, except that for the 100, you just went all out. The 100 was the first: I lined up at the blocks. When the gun went off all I saw was the backs of seven others pulling away from me. I gained traction and after a few steps turned on full speed. Much to my surprise I came in a comfortable first! The next race was the 220. I knew that this involved some pacing and strategy. My strategy was simple; run off Gordie's shoulder until I saw the finish line, then turn it up full blast. I finished well ahead of him in this race too. The 440 was something of a repeat and I won it handily. The other two events only got me a second and third place finish.

Following that afternoon, I was approached by the Director of Athletics, who sat me down and said, "Do

you know that you came within a fifth of
tying the Canadian record for the 220?"
that I could have run faster than I did. He wanted
me to join the football team. I was 6'2, 175 lbs and
fast. I told him I didn't know anything about football
but he said that it didn't matter, and that I would be
an all-star in my first year at University. Pretty heady
stuff.

However, in the previous months I had done some stage work, including a lead role in the high school play for which I won an award. The Director was Miss Robbins, a lovely lady who insisted that I stick to acting and forego the football. Then there was my mother who, I am sure, while very proud of my red ribbons, was just a tad worried about what athletics might do to my health. I ultimately chose acting over football. However, the question has always remained in my mind: suppose I had done what the coach had wanted me to? Suppose I had gone on and broken the Canadian record for the 220? Would I have gone on to Law School or would I have followed another career? And had I made that choice back in the spring of 1944, would I have ended up in Hamilton, a struggling young lawyer about to discover the word conservation?

1945

In the summer of 1945, I experienced a severe attack of appendicitis and was admitted to Grace

Hospital in Windsor. Apparently, the operation was rather difficult as I had not been properly prepped. That was because about midnight the night before a nurse came in my room to give me an enema. The trouble was, it turned out that we knew each other from school and both of us became very embarrassed. Holding the enema kit, she said to me, "You know what to do with this?" And I said, "Just leave it." She left and of course I did not get my enema. As a result, I was very ill after the surgery with excruciating gas pains.

Because I was so sick I had a full-time nurse in my private room. The night following surgery I heard a woman screaming "I'm gonna to kill the son of a bitch! I'm gonna kill the son of a bitch!" and the next thing I knew there was a woman in my room with what appeared to be a knife raised over her head. It turned out to be a pair of long scissors but I suppose they would have done the job as well. Fortunately, my nurse, who was a rather big lady, flew across the room and tackled this woman whereupon a vicious battle took place at the foot of my bed. The woman, who was eventually diagnosed with psychosis, was subdued and I was saved from being murdered at the tender age of 19. Incidentally, during my stay in hospital the United States dropped the bomb on Hiroshima and a week later on Nagasaki.

University Life

So, when I left for university in the fall of 1945, I was recovering from my appendix operation and my close call with murder. I had selected the University of Toronto, Victoria College, and was enrolled in the Honours Law program. For the next four years, my residence was in the all-male Burwash Hall in Middle House. My first year, I shared my room with my old friend Bill Young with whom I had gone to high school at Walkerville. My second year, I also had a roommate, Craig Armstrong, but in my third and fourth years I got my own private room, which had been originally occupied by Lester B. Pearson.

The population of the University increased substantially in 1945, jumping from about 6000 to approximately 25,000, the difference being the returning War veterans. I think because it was the first time many of us were away from home, university and university life was a place for good times. For the next several years, I engaged in what seemed like an endless party and where fun and practical jokes dominated the day as well as the night.

Tom, U. of T. days

For instance, there was an occasion when my house mates decided to move all my furniture from my room and set it up on the tennis court out on the quadrangle. I only spent one night there before having to return my belongings to the dorm. Another time in second year, I remember sitting in Diana Sweets restaurant. Two or three guys from Middle House dropped by my table suggesting I should go back to my room to see what was going on. Some engineering students in Middle House had acquired an aeronautical balloon which they set up on my bed and filled with water. The balloon held an enormous amount of water, bulging over the sides of my bed and down to the floor. Their plan had been to leave the balloon on my bed, with thumbtacks placed near the edge of the balloon. As they poured the last pail of water into the balloon, it burst, filling the room to the top of the baseboard; however, the water quickly seeped through the porous floor and into the room of the chap below. In my room, only the mattress and the floor was soaked. In his room, everything was soaked; and I mean everything. Even the ceiling globe was filled with water. I shook my head and offered to buy him a goldfish.

On another occasion, St. Michael's College, which was immediately adjacent to the Burwash residences, had just won a junior hockey tournament. They celebrated by firing some skyrockets, some of which came our way. We responded to this aggression with our own version of an arms race. I went out and bought a lot of quite powerful rockets. I had a long bazooka-like tube and the technical assistance of a returned army captain named John Nicol. John was an extremely serious and dour sort and did not approve of the antics of all us youngsters just out of high school. Despite that, he joined the retaliatory strike against St. Michael's. One rocket missed St. Michael's and crossed Bay St. narrowly missing a streetcar. Another rocket, went through a window at St. Mike's and exploded inside. At this point, the police arrived. It had been reported to police that a May Day riot was underway. Otherwise, nothing really came of it. We likely should have been expelled.

I Play Hitler

As I have told you, life in residence at Victoria College in those early years right after the war was great fun and pranks of one kind or another seemed like an everyday occurrence.

One day, I think it was probably in the spring of 1946, I got my hands on a German uniform and officer's cap and on the spur of the moment I decided to climb out on the open balcony at Middlehouse to do an imitation of Adolph Hitler making a speech. I did the thing in gibberish German, imitating as best I could the mannerisms of Hitler. There was a good crowd of students in the quadrangle at the time and as I went on with my speech the crowd swelled and periodically would chant "Sieg Heil". I'm told that these chants could be heard echoing across Queens Park. The well-known Canadian performer and fellow student at Victoria College, Don Harron, was in the crowd and he told me later that he thought my performance on the balcony imitating Hitler was the best performance I had ever done. It was so much fun. It was spontaneous and the sarcastic humour resonated with the students barely a year after the war ended when Hitler had become a bad memory.

Today the residences in Burwash Hall are all co-ed and the very model of proper decorum. In my days there, it was an all-male domain with more of an Animal House culture. It was a tradition in the men's residences that each spring there would be a "tapping" for the seniors who were graduating. This was sort of like a hazing. In fact, each house had its own planning committee for the senior's "tapping".

I remember the tapping of a senior by the name of Art Bailey. We rented a van for the occasion. I had a bag of feathers, actually a pillow that had come apart which I had kept knowing that it would have a useful purpose at some point. When we did the tapping, we grabbed Art from his bed in the middle of the night. He was dressed only in his underwear shorts. We had a large jar of honey and we managed to coat his entire body with the honey and then spread the feathers all over him. The feathers stuck quite well and he was a sight to behold: honeyed and feathered you might say.

We put him in the van and drove up to North Toronto to his girlfriend's home. We then tied him to a tree in front of her house. I think we caused a bit of a disturbance in the street and some neighbour called the police. The police did not catch up with us until we were back down at the corner of Avenue Road and Bloor Street near the Park Plaza Hotel. They led us back to the police station where we explained that this was all a college prank. They told us that they had had a fellow in there a little while before all covered with feathers and told us to get lost.

I wouldn't want to give you the impression that it was like this all the time in the men's residence. After all, the residence was filled with serious students: virtually all of them graduated and went on to distinguished careers of one kind or another. But we did have fun.

Because of the amount of time that was spent having fun instead of studying, I found that every spring I was in terror of failing. At the Law School, if you failed even one exam, you were out. So, between March and April, I would burn the midnight oil and try to catch up on all the work that I had neglected to do during the previous months.

Somehow, I managed to pass my exams in each of those four years, but perhaps not with great distinction. It was not until I got married in June 1949 that I found myself attending all my classes and doing my proper assignments. As a result, when I graduated with my LLB degree in 1950 I graduated with honours along with only two others. There was a big attrition rate at the school. My class, which had started out with about seventy-five students, ended with only about fifteen graduating.

I remember one of the things I used to do in my spare time while I was in Law School was to go down to the Law Courts in the Old City Hall in Toronto and watch some of Canada's greatest lawyers perform, people such as G. Arthur Martin and JJ Robinette. It was a wonderful opportunity to see the best legal minds at work!

Having been introduced to the world of the stage in high school at Walkerville Collegiate, it was not surprising that I would join the Victoria College Dramatic Society upon arriving at university. The play being performed that fall was Thornton Wilder's *The Skin of Our Teeth*.

I was told by other members of the Drama Club that freshmen did not get lead roles, and I remember specifically that Royce Frith, who later became a well-known Canadian senator, told me not to expect to get an important role in the play.

The director at that time, and for most of my years at university, was Dora Mavor Moore, a leader in Toronto theatre, after whom the Dora Awards is named. I remember reading for the part of Antrobus, the lead role. I was, I thought, dreadful and quite scared. At the end of the reading I remember Mrs. Moore saying, "You love the theatre, don't you?" So, contrary to everyone's expectations, including mine, I got the role! As it turned out, it was probably my best performance in any role while I was at university.

The next year found me cast in the lead role of Petruchio in Shakespeare's *Taming of The Shrew*. Shakespeare was really not my cup of tea. For one thing, apparently, I had picked up an American accent from growing up in the border city of Windsor. I remember I fell in love with my leading lady, Peggy Brown, who went on to be a well-known Canadian actress of stage and radio.

I never got over stage fright and I can tell you it is a very terrifying experience. But what would happen was, the moment I stepped on stage, and especially if my first line drew a laugh, the stage fright would disappear immediately. I was reassured about all of this by being told that many famous actors, for example, the actress Katherine Cornell, would throw up before going on stage every night.

At that time, I seriously considered making the stage my career. But then in a sober moment, I thought it might be more prudent to get my law degree before attempting a life in theatre. I think this was one of the wiser decisions I made about my life because for every successful actor there must be a thousand pretty good actors who are not. However, one of the unwise decisions I did make was to turn down an offer made to me by Dora Mavor Moore to take me under her wing for private tutelage to hone my skills in public speaking and oration. She thought that with my voice and manner of delivery, I had the potential to be a great public speaker.

In addition to the theatre, I participated every year in the famous Victoria College variety show called the Vic Bob. I even performed once on stage at Massey Hall, along with my fellow performer, Don Harron, who later became known to most Canadians as Charlie Farquarson, a beloved Canadian character, and also Norm Jewison of Hollywood fame. At one point, Norm Jewison and I performed a duet entitled *The TTC*. I knew that Norm was very talented but I had no idea that he would go on to direct such famous movies as *Moonstruck, Jesus Christ Superstar, In the Heat of the Night, Fiddler on the Roof* and many more.

A Lifeguard

In the summer of 1946, I took a job as a lifeguard at the East Windsor Bathing Beach. It does not exist anymore and for good reason. It consisted of a huge covered pavilion, with a long, wide wooden pier that extended about 150 feet out to the navigable channel of the Detroit River, where the water moved about three or four miles an hour and was about twenty feet deep.

The water had a visibility of about one foot. That meant if you did not see what we called a "sinker" go under, then the chances were that he or she would drown. It was a very stressful job but the good news is that in the 20 years it operated, not one person was lost to drowning. But I must tell you, it was nerve-wracking knowing that the lives of people we didn't know were resting in our hands most of the time. We did get to know about certain people who could be a liability though and we always kept a special eye on them. I remember there was one kid we called the perpetual sinker and we were always pulling him out of the water.

Anyway, I survived that summer, although I did have an altercation with a member of the notorious Detroit Purple Gang on the dock and he threatened to come back and do me in. As a result, the Windsor Police had to put a special guard at the gate of the bathing beach to protect me for the rest of the summer.

Lifeguard Tom with Joe watching over, 1946

Canoe Lake

I didn't have a job in the summer of 1947. I remember that in July my father went on a fishing trip in northern Quebec. My mother decided to take her own vacation at Grandview Farms, a resort near Huntsville in the Muskoka area of Ontario. I told her I would go with her. While there, we decided we would pay a visit to my Uncle KC on Canoe Lake in Algonquin Park. His cottage was not far from the Portage Store and accessible only by boat. After he picked us up at the dock, he took us on a tour of the lake. I recall passing in front of Camp Ahmek, which is the boys' camp of the Taylor Statten Camps. It was then I noticed a very good looking blonde woman walking across the beach in front of the pavilion. I decided then and there this might be a good place to try and find a job. Normally, it would not be possible to get on staff at Taylor Statten without having a lot of camp experience, particularity at Ahmek. I had not had any similar experience except for those few weeks as a camper each summer at Camp Kitchekwana.

However, as luck would have it, a counsellor in the intermediate section had to go home quite suddenly and Tay (Taylor's son) Statten needed to replace him right away. I got the job. I discovered I had six 12 and 13-year-old boys who were a rather disparate group and one of them was subject to almost constant bullying by the others because he was a bed-wetter. However, I was able to get them ready for what would be their very first canoe trip in the Park. Actually, this was also my first trip in the Park. The trip took us from Canoe Lake up to the northern end of the Park via a number of rivers and lakes to Cedar Lake. It turned out to be a difficult trip for boys of that age but they endured and it became an experience of a lifetime for all of us. I saw these young boys grow up before my eyes into young men, showing a level of responsibility and maturity that I had not anticipated.

At Taylor Statten camp, the kids were supposed to plan their own canoe trip with the help of their counsellor and that's what happened with my kids. They wanted to go on a trip to Brent which was right at the northern end of the Park. Now nobody had told me this was a trip for seniors, not for intermediates. Anyway, the boys planned it, we registered our trip with the tripping office, prepared all our gear and supplies and off we went. It was apparent after the first day they were never going to make it to Brent and back within a week. By the end of the second day we were already a full day behind. I told the boys we would have to change our plans as Brent was too far and we had to make it a shorter trip.

When I woke up the next morning and climbed out of my tent I found the boys already up and sitting around the campfire looking very glum. I said, "What's the matter?" and they looked at me and said, "Tommy, we want to go to Brent," and I said, "Well, that is going to be very difficult: you'll have to work very hard and miss things like lunch". I thought that would deter them but it didn't, so the decision was made they would push on for Brent no matter how difficult it was. I admired their determination and so we continued on and about four o'clock we arrived at the end of a portage where the Petawawa River flows into Cedar Lake. This was a very long portage that cut across the bottom of a U in the river. With a portage that long, it did not take any intelligence to realize the river was impossible to navigate by canoe. I knew the rules were that the kids were supposed to camp by 4 o'clock but they were all determined to press on and finish their journey to Brent, which they could see across the lake. I still didn't want to impede their enthusiasm and I looked long and hard at the lake and saw it was flat calm. I decided it would be safe to cross.

My canoe had one camper in the bow, my CIT had two campers in his canoe and the third canoe held three campers. The other two canoes apparently were well balanced but as it turned out my canoe was a bit light in the bow. As we got out some distance in the lake, all of a sudden, a very strong westerly wind came up and the lake became strewn with whitecaps. It is not good to have whitecaps coming broadside to your canoe and I was very fearful that one or all of us might swamp. As we proceeded in the high wind, to my dismay my canoe was being pushed towards the East while the other two canoes were able to maintain their course. I put all my strength and power into trying turn my bow up towards the wind but with my rather weak paddler in the bow it was impossible.

However, despite it being a very rough crossing, we all made it safely to the north shore, although my canoe ended up several hundred yards east of the other two. It turns out, on that afternoon, the Director of Tripping for Taylor Statten was in the ranger station at Brent. They had looked out over the lake and saw the whitecaps and said well we're not gonna see any more canoes on the lake today when at that point they spotted our three struggling to reach the shore. The kids were ecstatic to have reached their destination and soon descended on the little tuck shop at the railway stop. The trip home was uneventful and I had a very happy group of boys on my hands as they had achieved something they thought they would not be able to do.

While we were away, the office at Taylor Statten received a telephone call from the ranger station at Brent to report that a couple of counsellors and a camper from Camp Ahmek had been killed in the rapids on the Petawawa River just south of Cedar Lake. Apparently, an accident had happened and an aircraft had overflown the site and mistook two demolished Camp Arowhon canoes floating in the water below the rapids for Ahmek canoes.

One of the ironies is that that call was taken by Joan, the woman who was to become my wife a couple of years later. Apparently, what had happened was that there was a Camp Arowhon canoe trip close to where we had been on the Petawawa at about the same time we were there and when they reached the long portage on the river, decided they were going to walk two of the canoes along the edge of the rapids, a monumentally stupid thing to do. The canoes were swept from their hands and down the rapids. Apparently, the three counsellors then found a ranger cabin and went to sleep.

Meanwhile, the rest of the Arowhon trippers had taken the portage and seeing their canoes at the bottom of the rapids reported the incident at Brent Ranger Station. That was when the rangers flew over the site and mistook the Arowhon canoes for ours. I later saw the two canoes and there was hardly a rib that was not broken: it was though a monster had mashed them up in its hands.

Ghosts, Stones and Bones

As I said earlier, I even had an encounter with the ghost of Tom Thomson one foggy, moonlit night on Canoe Lake. I really do not believe in ghosts now and I didn't then. But anyone who has ever spent time on Canoe Lake knows well that the ghost of Tom Thomson exists and still paddles the quiet waters in the wee small hours, sitting in the stern seat, pipe in mouth, and fedora snapped down.

Every night after we got the kids tucked away, many of the counsellors would get together and have a late-night campfire — no booze, just singing and good conversation. One night, about two in the morning, I was returning to Camp Ahmek after dropping off my then girlfriend at Camp Wapameo. There was a clear sky, a full moon, with an iridescent layer of fog lying above the glassy surface of the water. I was in my canoe, navigating by the moon, using the silent stroke so as to avoid breaking the magical quiet of the night. Suddenly, out of the mist, a canoe appeared on my right on a collision course. I stopped paddling, heart pounding, as this silent canoe with the figure of a man, pipe in mouth, fedora snapped down, passed directly in front of me and disappeared into the mist. Neither of us spoke. He left nothing but the ripples of his canoe. The encounter scared the hell out of me, and I must say that I have never forgotten it.

It is strange for me to be able to say that I knew someone who knew Tom Thomson. His name was Mark Robinson. He had been a Park Ranger during the Thomson years in Algonquin Park and was his very close, if not best, friend. When Mark Robinson retired, Taylor Statten gave him a cabin to live in on the grounds of Camp Ahmek on Canoe Lake. It was while Robinson was living there that I met him in the summer of 1947 when I was on staff at the Camp. I had the opportunity to chat with him a few times but my best recollection was his story about the burial and exhumation of Thomson's body from the Mowat cemetery out on Canoe Lake. It's a tiny place and only about three people are buried there.

Apparently, Tom Thomson's family in Owen Sound wanted him to be buried in the family plot in his hometown. They hired an undertaker from Huntsville to recover his body. When the undertaker arrived with a metal casket, he strangely refused all help to dig up the body. According to Mark Robinson, he went to the cemetery at night by himself. In the morning he showed up at the Canoe Lake train station with a sealed coffin on a horse-drawn wagon. Robinson was there and he told me he helped load the coffin onto the baggage car of the train. He said that when they lifted up the casket to slide it onto the floor of the baggage car he could hear rocks tumbling from one end of the box to the other. He told me he knew then Thomson's body was not in that casket and it further explained to him why the undertaker had not wanted any assistance to dig up a putrid body.

The Thomson family in Owen Sound has always refused permission to dig up the grave to see what is in the casket. However, if that should ever happen, and if Mark Robinson was telling me the truth, then what you would find in the box would be stones, not bones.

The Thomson death on Canoe Lake in July 1917 remains one of Canada's most intriguing mysteries. I rather hope that it remains so. It has already generated many books, some more authoritative than others, and all with their own theories as to how Thomson met his end and where his bones lie today.

Joan

I discovered that the girl I first spotted on the beach was named Joan Baden-Powell, but during that summer I hardly got to know her at all. In fact, she paid no attention to me whatsoever. After Labour Day, at the end of the season, the Camp runs "September Camp" for alumni campers and staff and I was kept on to help entertain the guests. It was not until near the end of camp that I had the courage to ask Joan to go sailing. I remember going to the sailing dock where many dinghies were tied up side by side, bow towards the dock. I jumped onto the small deck of one of them, intending of course to swing into the cockpit but I hesitated, grabbed the mast and immediately capsized the boat. Joan recalls me coming to the surface with my sandals floating on each side of my head. It was rather ignominious beginning to a romance.

Summer 1948

Jasper Park Lodge was operated by the Canadian National Railway and owned by the Government of Canada. I was able to get a job through the patronage of Paul Martin Senior who was our Member of Parliament and a Federal Cabinet Minister. My job was as a driver of one of the glass-topped tour buses at the Lodge.

Not long after I arrived I began to see how incompetently the Lodge was operated. I started out driving staff between the Lodge and the Town of Jasper. That did not involve any mountain driving and in fact, I had had virtually no training in that regard. One of the tours offered was to Mount Edith Cavell and the Angel Glacier. This involved a drive of several miles up a very treacherous road that included four 180° switchbacks, which could be easily negotiated by car but buses had to shuttle back and forth two or three times to make each turn. The road was narrow and unpaved with no trees alongside to hide the drop-offs so you just looked out into nothingness. Adding to the stress, was my life-long fear of heights. My only training on the road was once as a passenger, which for me was a white-knuckle ride.

Early in the summer, the dispatcher asked me if I could take a busload of passengers up to Mount Edith Cavell. As I recall it was a load of Canadian insurance people. As the bus started up the road, a woman sitting behind me started screaming. This was a bit unnerving for a novice driver and I should've had the good sense to find a way to get her off the bus then and there. On the first switchback I approached, I made the initial turn into the rock-face, put the bus into what I thought was forward gear and allowed it to roll back on the brakes.

Unfortunately, the forward gear and reverse gear were next to each other and I had unknowingly put the bus into reverse. I released the brake and hit the gas, expecting to go forward but instead backed up until my rear wheels hit the wooden guardrail. The back end of the bus was suspended out in space. The woman behind me went totally hysterical and I could hardly blame her. I was scared out of my mind as well. After I figured out what I had done wrong, I was able to complete the turn successfully. I negotiated the next three switchbacks and drove to my destination at the end of the road where I found a taxi to take the screaming lady safely back to the Lodge.

Many years later, in the 1990s I drove the road again with my wife, Meralee, only to find it was paved, lined with mature forest which blocked out the void beside the road that I so vividly remembered and no longer had any switchbacks or dangerous drop-offs. I had told her this story and I think she wondered what I was talking about. It was now really quite a tame drive.

On another occasion I took a busload of people, who turned out to be Mormons from Salt Lake City, to a place called Miette Hot Springs. It was about a seven-mile drive up a grade to the Hot Springs; no switchbacks but very windy. I had never been up there before. Coming back down, I was in a lower gear and touching the brake occasionally to check my speed. No one had told me of the dangers of touching my brake going down these mountain roads or warned me about the possibility of their overheating and possibly failing. Suddenly, I realized I had no brakes at all! I started gaining speed but did not dare to gear down again because I was afraid I would end up in neutral, unable to get into a lower gear. We did get down safely, albeit rather quickly, and I remember the Mormon passengers thought it was a really fun ride down the hill, not realizing that it was not intended to be that way at all.

The Manager of the Lodge was a chain-smoking alcoholic incompetent. There were 400 people on staff and on one occasion 250 of them became deathly ill with food poisoning. Some doctors visiting at the Lodge found that the staff was being served unrefrigerated food that was fly infested and ordered the Manager not to give the staff that kind of food any longer. I myself did not get sick but that was because as a driver I was able to eat all my meals in town except for breakfast. The whole incident was another example of what I considered to be incompetent management.

On the other hand, my job at Jasper was one of the best summers of my life. With about 400 people on staff, most of them university students, I realized there was an opportunity here to put together a staff show, which had never been done at Jasper. My friend Norman Jewison with whom I had performed at the University of Toronto, was the producer of the staff show at the Banff Springs Hotel. So, I became the producer of the Jasper show and it was, if I may say so, a very delightful production, and many tourists who saw both of them claimed ours was the better show. One of the songs written for our show was called Jasper Blues and Bing Crosby, who was a frequent guest at the Lodge, later sang the song on his national radio show in the US.

The previous fall, I had started to date Joan and I missed her very much. I remember telephoning her and telling her to come out and that somehow I would find her a job at the Lodge. She did and ended up working in the gift shop. Our romance flourished and one evening sitting on a small hill I asked her to marry me and she accepted. Well, the next day I went back to the site to see where the engagement had happened and found that we had been sitting on a large mound of rotted manure which was waiting to be spread on the Lodge gardens! What a romantic!

There is one other thing I want to mention about my summer at Jasper. One evening when I was in the main lodge I spotted Dr. Harold Fox, who was a guest there. He had been my professor at the Law School the previous year for a course in copyrights and patents. When we were to take our final exam, he told us it would be a three-hour exam rather than the usual two and a half hours and that we could take any material we wanted into the exam. This sounded ominous to me.

When I went to write the exam, I read the examination paper carefully before starting to answer the questions. We were asked to answer four out of eight questions, all questions having equal value. Reading it over, I realized that four of the questions were ridiculously simple while the other four would require complicated essay type answers. After thinking about the fact that Dr. Fox was a successful lawyer, I wondered why he would expect us to answer the difficult questions.

So, I answered the four easy ones and was finished my three-hour exam in about thirty minutes. I looked around and saw most of the other students writing furiously but after satisfying myself that I had followed the instructions carefully, I left. After returning to my residence I wondered if I had made a mistake.

When I spotted Dr. Fox in the lobby I decided to ask him about the exam. He asked me what mark I had received and I told him a first. He said, "So, you answered the four simple questions". He said he had not expected any of the class would actually practise law in the field of copyrights and patents: he just wanted to see which of us would make good lawyers. It was a life lesson for me. When there is a simple and direct way of doing something choose that route and not the difficult and hazardous one.

Tom and Joan, Jasper, 1948

As a footnote to the Jasper stories, I was returning with my family from Quebec City to Ancaster on New Year's Eve some years later and I decided to take them to the Mount Royal Hotel, a fine hotel in downtown Montreal, rather than to a motel on the highway. Early the next morning before continuing home, we went down to the lobby to have breakfast. The lobby and the very upscale restaurant that was open for breakfast appeared empty. As we entered the restaurant, the Maître D' quietly told me that they would be unable to serve my wife, Joan. "Why is that?" I asked. "Because she is improperly attired," he told me.

Joan was wearing a very expensive pantsuit that I had bought her for Christmas in a swanky store in Yorkville. Pantsuits were a recent fashion trend and all the rage for women in those days. To say that I was enraged was to put it mildly. When I got home I wrote to the hotel manager expressing my outrage in no uncertain terms. I later received a letter of humble apology from the manager. And who was that manager? None other than the chain-smoking, alcoholic incompetent who managed Jasper Park Lodge in the summer of 48!

Summer 1949

In the summer 1949, I married Joan at Saint Thomas Anglican Church in Toronto. We set off to cottage country in my family's car for our honeymoon. Part of my mission while there was to find a site for my parents to build a family cottage. Ironically, of all the places we could find, our search took us back to Lake Nosbonsing, where we had, as a family, camped in the early 1930s. And I found a site across the lake from Big Moose Camp! The price in those days was $2.00 a foot and we purchased about 500 feet of frontage on the water and proceeded to have a cottage erected. The cottage roof and sides were covered with cedar shakes which were brought in by train from British Columbia. Sadly, the cottage burned down several years later when a sonic boom, caused by a jet flying low overhead, separated the stove pipe where it passed through the attic of the cottage. My parents escaped in just their nightclothes, saving only "Tex", a wooden cowboy statue I had bought for them in Jasper a few years earlier. As the cottage was built out of all that nice dry cedar, it was indeed a spectacular fire which apparently could be seen all the way to North Bay, some twenty-five miles away. The cottage was rebuilt and continued to be enjoyed by the family until it was eventually sold in the mid 70's.

1950 — We Go West

Long before I graduated from high school I knew I wanted to be a lawyer. At that time the process was to get an undergraduate degree in anything and then go on to Osgoode Hall for three years. Osgoode Hall was operated by the Law Society of Upper Canada.

The Law Society was not a university and had no power to grant degrees. However, there was a law school at the University of Toronto where I could enrol in the honours law course for four years and obtain an undergraduate degree in law. This seemed like a good idea to me as I thought it would give me something of a leg up when I attended Osgoode.

As I was approaching the end of my fourth year at the University of Toronto law school, the long simmering feud over legal education between the University and the Law Society was coming to a boil. The University was demanding the Law Society give up its monopoly on legal education in the province. At that time the University of Toronto Law degree was recognized in every English-speaking jurisdiction around the world except Ontario. I was certain that recognition would happen soon so I decided to enter my fifth year at the University and obtain my LLB degree.

That meant that with one more year of university I would be able to be qualified for a call to the Bar in Ontario. Unfortunately, my prediction about recognition was only partly correct. It was indeed granted but not made retroactive. So, there I was with five years of law school and two degrees in law and I was faced with the prospect of having to go to Osgoode Hall and start all over again, which would have meant a total of eight years in law school, something I was not prepared to do. I decided to head to Calgary where I had some connections. So, in the early summer of 1950, Joan and I went to Alberta where I was soon called to the Bar and where I found my first employment in my field. As a matter of interest there are now six university-based law schools in Ontario; at the Universities of Windsor, Ottawa, Toronto, Queens, Western, and York, which is where Osgoode ended up.

I had the possible advantage of being the nephew of the former Chief Justice of Alberta, William Ives, and I was able to land a job with Harry Nolan, K.C. who was with the firm as it was then called, Nolan, Chambers, Might, Saucier, Peacock and Jones. This was the first firm of R.B. Bennett and is still a major international law firm known today as Bennett Jones.

Tom and Joe, Calgary, 1950

Tom with Joan, Calgary, 1950

My first job with Mr. Nolan was to assist him in a trial that was going on in Western Canada. It became known as the Bread Combines Case. The largest bakeries in the four western provinces had conspired together to eliminate competition and raise the price of bread incrementally over time. This was indeed a criminal conspiracy. However, none of the actual conspirators, that is to say the executives of these companies, were ever charged with anything. It was only their corporate employers that were charged. Working on this trial influenced me over the course of my life as I found that corporate executives could enter into serious crime and never be charged: only the companies that employ them were charged. The combines case lasted over 100 days and not one of the corporate executives appeared in the courtroom or faced cross-examination. The companies eventually pleaded guilty and paid fines ranging from about $5000-$25,000, a mere pittance. This social injustice had an enormous impact on me. That's when I realized that the rules of the game protect corporate executives from responsibility for their crimes. It is somewhat ironic as I write this that there is a similar story in the Canadian news these days. Some things never change!

Although working for Mr. Nolan was very interesting and enlightening it was not giving me the breadth of law experience which I felt I needed. As a result, after a few months I switched firms and joined Scott and Gregg, a much smaller firm which I thought might give me a broader exposure to the Law. One of the firm's clients was the Calgary Associate Clinic and not long after joining the firm I was given the job of conducting my very first trial: collect one of the Clinic's unpaid medical bills. These were pre-medicare days and a gynaecologist at the Clinic had performed an operation on a farmer's wife. When the fee of $142 was not paid, the clinic sued the farmer for the amount. The trial was to be held in the prairie town of Trochu, about an hour and a half's drive from Calgary. My boss Colonel Scott had given me his new maroon Buick and I was to pick up the doctor and the judge and drive them to the trial. That didn't seem quite right to me but I was hardly in any position to argue the optics of the situation.

It was spring melt time and it seemed that most of southern Alberta was under water. The main street of Trochu was pretty much sloppy mud. We went into the court clerk's office where the trial was to take place and discovered the defendant was not there. The judge asked the clerk if the defendant had received the Notice of Trial. He didn't know so the judge sent him off to the post office to find out if it had been delivered. It turned out it had not, due to the poor road conditions. The judge asked me to phone the defendant to see whether he would come to the trial if he was picked up. When I spoke to the defendant he said he would be willing to come but it was not possible due to the bad roads. The judge wanted me to go and pick them up anyway. So, I set out again in my boss's beautiful Buick, which by now had become pretty much encased in mud. I followed the directions to the defendant's farmhouse. Unlike Ontario where farmhouses are built close to the road, in Alberta they were usually placed closer to the centre of the farmer's large acreage so the laneways to their houses were very long.

On my way to the farmhouse, I came to an area on the road that was under water for about the length of a football field. I began to understand why the farmer's mail had not been delivered. And as I stared at the water in front of me and wondered whether I could drive through it, I noticed that on each side of the road there were fence posts which gave me a pretty good idea of the depth of the water. I decided I could make it. Eventually, I found the farmer's lane and turned into it. I then understood why he could not get out as there was a river running across the top of his laneway from one field to the other and it was clearly impossible to get through it by car. The farmer showed up at the other side of this cascade and we shouted back and forth.

I then had the brilliant idea of him coming out on his tractor. He said his tractor had not been operated since the fall and did not have a battery so I suggested he transfer the battery from his car to his tractor and he said he would. He disappeared back into the barn for some time and then finally reappeared driving a large open single-seat tractor and headed towards the laneway. As he crossed the deep rushing water it was a sight I will never forget. Mounted on his shoulders was his wife! The big tractor passed easily through the water and the two of them climbed into the new Buick, dragging in even more mud.

We then proceeded back towards Trochu, passing through the football field of water again and finally arrived rather late in the day for the trial. I must say I wish I had a transcript of the trial as it was in retrospect perhaps one of the funniest days I have ever experienced in court. It turned out the operation had something to do with his wife's private parts and his main complaint seemed to be about their ensuing sex life and that is why he did not want not pay the bill. The trial did not take very long and at the end of the day I had my first court-won judgement for the large sum of $142.00.

I then drove the farmer and his wife back home, passing again through the same lake on the same road. The last I saw of them, he was driving the tractor back up the lane to the farm, with his wife mounted on his shoulders, waving goodbye. I then drove back to Trochu, passing through the lake on the road for the fourth time, where I picked up the judge and my client. We then proceeded back to Calgary, arriving somewhere around midnight. What a day my first trial had been! In my thirty-seven years as a lawyer, having spent endless hours in court, nothing has ever come close to this experience. I don't think I saw the humour in the situation then because I was a really young and very nervous lawyer at the time.

Coming to Hamilton

Two years later, on a cold July day when we stood on 8th Avenue watching the Stampede Parade, it started to snow! I said to Joan, "I don't want to live any place where there is any possibility of snow in July". And so, not long after, we headed home to Ontario. I was able to get my call to the Bar in Ontario because I was a Barrister and Solicitor of the Province of Alberta in good standing. The problem facing us was in what city or town should we settle. Toronto was too big and crowded and I didn't want to go back to Windsor. But Hamilton, my ancestral home, seemed just right. Sort of sounds like the story of the Three Bears.

I recall sitting on a gravestone in a cemetery across the bay from the city looking at its skyline and thinking, what amazing place; a split-level city with an escarpment running through it, a big bay at its foot and two magnificent valleys at each end, located near the Niagara fruit belt and adjacent to some of the world's best agricultural land. I thought Hamilton had it all.

So that was it — Hamilton it was to be. I found a position with the law firm of Treleaven and Milne whose offices were in the old Birk's Building in downtown Hamilton. Although the firm did mainly commercial law, I also did the occasional criminal law case. In February, 1953, I happened to be at the old Barton Street Jail in Hamilton to see a client and experienced an event which I have never forgotten.

The Hanging of Harry Lee

About a week earlier, a man named Harry Lee was hanged at the Jail. He had been convicted the previous June of the murder of Mary Rosenblatt. She was found shot to death in a car owned by Lee at the side of the road near Sheffield, on Highway 8 near Hamilton. He was also found in the car with a gunshot wound, as was a 22-caliber rifle. It seemed like an open and shut case and he was charged with her murder. However, he had maintained from the beginning he was innocent, saying she had been murdered by two men who had abducted them both.

Harry Lee's mother was black and his father was Hispanic. He worked as a caretaker at a synagogue on Cannon Street in Hamilton and that is where he likely met Mary. She was a married woman and the mother of two young children. They had become lovers and had had a relationship for some period of time. The trial became a sensation in Hamilton. The Crown Attorney was Harvey McCulloch, QC, a brilliant, well experienced prosecutor. Lee was represented by two young lawyers trying their first murder case, John Agro and Gerry Kennedy.

Lee testified at his trial, maintaining the story that he and Mary had been victims of the two men, but at the end of the trial the jury found him guilty. In accordance with the law at that time, he was sentenced to be hanged. The presiding judge of the trial was Mr. Justice Wishart Spence. Lee was remanded to the old Barton Street jail to await his hanging which was scheduled for February 3. Apparently, the trial and the circumstances surrounding the case aroused a considerable amount of public outcry for clemency for Harry but nothing worked and on February 3, shortly after midnight, he was hanged.

About a week after that, I was there to interview a client. Coincidentally, another young Hamilton lawyer by the name of John Bowlby was at the jail that morning for the same reason. We decided we wanted to see where the hanging had taken place and so we went to visit the governor of the jail, whose name was John David Heddle. He was more than willing to talk about the event.

As we sat in his office, he described in great detail what had happened that night and the hours leading up to the hanging. Lee's solitary jail cell was located only steps away from the governor's office. During the months that Harry Lee was there, the governor got to know him quite well and found him to be a gentle and soft-spoken man. It was clear the governor had developed a fondness for Lee. He told us about having received the news from the Minister of Justice the day before the hanging was to take place that there would be no clemency and that the execution would proceed as scheduled.

When they say the next day what they really mean is as shortly after midnight as is possible on the day of the execution. That meant that all executions in Canada took place in the middle of the night. The executioners were hired by the Federal Government in what was a very secretive process. Obviously, being an executioner was not a full-time job so I assume they were paid for each job they did. Their identity was a closely guarded secret. The executioner, who was traditionally known as Mr. Ellis, could be your neighbour, your local grocer or your handyman. He could have been anyone from within the community.

Hangings in Canada were something of a ceremonial event. They were not only attended by those who were required to carry out the hanging but also by various other officials, including the sheriff of the county. In this case, the sheriff was Dr. Caldwell, a retired Hamilton dentist, who upon retirement was appointed the patronage job of sheriff. Little did he know that as part of his duties he would be required to participate in the ritualized legal killing of a man he did not know.

The hangman had arrived at the jail earlier in the evening. Shortly before midnight the governor, a minister and a couple of guards entered Lee's cell. Lee extended his hands so they could be shackled. As the governor told us the story, we followed the steps that Harry would have taken. We exited from his cell and out a nearby door into the jail yard, an area perhaps 50 feet square and surrounded by a high stone wall. Harry was in bare feet and it was a cold night with a skiff of snow on the ground. Off to the right, they could see the newly dug grave awaiting Harry's body. Partway across the yard, Harry stopped and looked up at the sky and said, "It's a beautiful night, Governor." At this point, the governor said he broke down and began to sob and fell back in the procession and someone else stepped forward to walk with Harry. They entered through a door in the middle of one of the stone walls and on the right was the scaffold with its traditional thirteen steps. Harry walked up unaided and in silence.

When they reached the top of the scaffold, Harry walked a few steps and stood on the trap door. The hangman placed a noose around his neck and then bent down to place a thong around his legs. At this point, the minister was reciting, "Yea, though I walk through the valley of the shadow of death...". The hangman then reached out and kicked the lever and the trap door sprung open, dropping Harry to his death.

As the governor was relating these details to us, he himself pulled the lever and the trap door fell open, allowing me to look into the newly whitewashed illuminated chamber below. I immediately saw it was heavily blood stained. I asked the Governor why there was so much blood and he said that the rope had cut an artery in Harry's neck and blood had spewed all over. He said the coroner immediately went down and checked to make sure that Harry was deceased. When he put his stethoscope on Harry's chest he found his heart was still beating and waited a bit and checked again. It was still beating. He did this several times. It took seven minutes for Harry's heart to stop. Harry Lee had not died instantly from a broken neck but had strangled to death. Such is the barbarity of capital punishment. Canada got rid of capital punishment in the 1960s and hopefully we will never see its return.

I can't recall exactly how I heard this story or if it is even true, but it is an interesting conclusion to the story of Harry Lee. In the mid 1970s, the Barton Street Jail was torn down and a new jail built in its place. There were seven bodies buried in the old jail yard, including that of Harry Lee, which were to be reinterred. The jail guard that dug up his body had been the very one that had buried Lee in February 1953, throwing lime on his body to help to dissolve it. But when he dug up Harry he found that the lime had indeed dissolved the bottom half but the top half, including his head had been well preserved in the tannin-rich soil. He was even able to recognize his face. I have not been able to determine where Lee's body was ultimately buried.

Ed Shaker, My First Law Partner

After two or three years at Treleaven and Milne, I decided to form my own firm with my old friend Ed Shaker. Ed and I had been classmates and friends since I started law school in 1945. The new office that Ed and I rented was in the Sun Life Building in the suite of Harold Minden, a very well-respected Hamilton lawyer who became something of a mentor to me. The space consisted of two very small side-by-side offices which were separated by a partition that was constructed of wood paneling up to about chair height, and above that was frosted glass, ending with a clear glass section at the top.

Ed had a client he had told me about; a young woman, mother of a small child, who was seeing him about her violent boyfriend. She had told Ed that he must be putting Spanish fly in her coffee because every time he came over she would end up in bed with him. Ed's advice to her was to stop drinking the coffee. However, on a much more serious note, he also told her to leave town as there was no way of making her safe otherwise.

One afternoon, she had an appointment to see Ed and I decided I wanted to have a look at her. So, while they were in the Ed's office I crawled up on top of my desk and slowly and quietly crept hand over hand up the frosted glass to the clear glass section and looked over. And to my horror, there staring up at me were both Ed and his client. I quickly dropped back down more embarrassed than I had ever been. I had neglected to turn out my ceiling light and so my silhouette had shown every inch of my crawl up the frosted glass wall.

The sad and awful part of the story is that shortly thereafter, the boyfriend went to her house and, while her landlady was holding her young child in her arms, he shot and killed the young mother. I tell you this story not only because of the humorous situation when I peeked over the wall, but also to emphasize the amount of violence against women I saw during my practice as a lawyer and certainly later during my time as a judge in Family Court.

As a side note, Ed Shaker is the first cousin of Ralph Nader and so I got know him and his remarkable family through Ed. It was Ralph that made me stop smoking and for that, I am forever grateful to him.

Tom, Ralph Nader and Ed Shaker, circa 1982

Last Trial in the Old Courthouse

About 1955, I was about to start a trial in the old courthouse on Princess Square. The presiding judge was Mr. Justice Stewart of the High Court of Ontario. He discovered this was to be the last trial to be held in the old 19th century courthouse before it was to be torn down and a new one built. He thought it was a historic occasion and ordered a delay in the start of my trial and asked the Court Clerk to find a photographer and to gather as many lawyers as he could find in and around the courthouse to come in for a historic photograph. It is interesting to note that the sheriff in the picture is Dr. Caldwell, the same sheriff and retired dentist that had been part of the official execution party for Harry Lee in 1953.

I have found this photograph to be rather fascinating for a number of years. For at least 10 years, I have been able to predict with absolute certainty who the next person in the photograph to die will be. How would I know this, you may ask? If you have not already guessed it is because I am the only person in the photograph who is still living. I hope I will be able to say this for many years to come.

Last trial day in the old Victorian courthouse before demolition, circa 1955.

Moving to Ancaster

The first place Joan and I found to live in Hamilton was a tiny one-bedroom walk-up on Concession Street above a theatre. It was dreadful but at least we saw every movie that came out. Shortly after, we found an apartment on Mountain Brow Boulevard, on the edge of the escarpment with a view over the City and across the lake to Toronto. That was 1952, and in November, our first child John Thomas Baden was born down the street at Nora Henderson Hospital. We still lived there when our second child, Elizabeth Ann was born in November of 1954. Before our third and last child, Mary Josephine was born in July 1958 we had moved into an old stone house in Ancaster, owned by Bill and Mary Balfour, on Wilson Street at Academy beside the old stone hotel. These are some of the oldest buildings in Ancaster which, fortunately, are still there.

I remember my father telling me about coming up from Hamilton in a horse drawn carriage to have a beer at that old hotel. We lived across the street and became friendly neighbours with the well-known Canadian artist Frank Pannabaker. His home is now a fine dining restaurant called Rousseau House.

Tom, John, Joan and Elizabeth, Ancaster, Ontario, 1955

I Become a Fireman

Right beside our house was a Shell gas station owned and operated by Tommy Beach, who was also the Fire Chief. He kept the fire engine there and that gave me the chance to fulfill a boyhood dream.

I became a volunteer fireman. It is hard to imagine a more poorly equipped Fire Department than Ancaster had at that time. Everything was antiquated: there was no radio communication of any description. When proceeding to a fire, only one firefighter was able to sit in the cab with the driver while the rest of us had to stand on a platform at the back of the truck, holding on for dear life!

I remember one cold winter night heading west on Highway 2 towards Brantford when I saw the whole western sky glowing from what I could only assume was a barn fire. In a barn fire, saving the barn was never possible — the task was to try to save the surrounding buildings. I do remember on one occasion, however, the volunteers going into the lower section of a burning barn to drive out as much of the farmer's equipment as was possible. How insane was that! Fortunately, after I got on Council I was able to find money in the Township budget to buy two new up-to-date fire trucks.

Part 2

My Public Life Begins

Town Council

It was while we were living in that house on Wilson Street that I took my first step into public affairs. I guess that somehow I had become known in Ancaster (I had opened a little part-time law office there in the house). A phone call came one night while we were having dinner. It was a prominent Ancaster resident named Ozzie Dutton, calling to tell me that I should run for Township Council. I said I would think about it. "Well," he said, "you don't have much time to think, it is already 7 o'clock and the meeting is at 8." I agreed to attend the meeting but nothing more. I came home that night as a nominee for Council.

I can no longer remember why I did that, maybe it was just ego. Anyway, I ended up getting my first taste of being a candidate for public office. I think I liked it. The next thing I knew, I was a councillor for the Township of Ancaster. Wilfred Wade was the Reeve and Bill Dunhum was the Deputy Reeve. I remained on Council for 7 years: 2 years as a councillor, and then in 1959, I was elected Deputy Reeve and member of the Wentworth County Council. And so, began my life of public service.

First Days on Council

I really do not recall much of my earliest days on Council, likely because we dealt with mundane matters such as roads and policing and God knows what other stuff that busies rural and suburban municipalities. I do remember one of the first things I did was to convince my four fellow councillors that the wealthy suburb of Ancaster needed to have a fire department equipped with an emergency vehicle with all the standard life saving equipment.

The irony of this story is that in the first week after we took delivery of that truck its very first emergency call was to our new home we had recently had built on the Old Dundas Road. My youngest child, Mary-Jo, who was three or four months old, had come frighteningly close to suffocating in her crib. The new emergency vehicle responded in minutes and whisked her off to hospital. Fortunately, she had no ongoing negative consequences from that nightmarish experience but the incident has always remained in my memory as one of the most traumatic times in my life. I never got over thinking that because I was elected to Council and did a good thing, a child's life had been saved, in this case, my own. I was learning early on that even a young councillor on Township Council could do important and meaningful things. It was not all potholes and budgets.

That was a period when the urban and rural parts of Ancaster almost came to blows over education; the rural one room school versus the modern eight room school. The supporters of each concept fought long and loud, much of it at our Council meetings, for it lay in our hands as to whether the two school boards should be merged to create the modern system we have today. It is likely hard for readers to imagine how bitter the fight was and the amount of animosity that was created. Imagine having to have police standing by at Council meetings when its chambers were jammed with opposing forces ready to resort to violence.

It turned out that serving on the Township Council provided a never-ending series of challenges, big and small, to stave off any tendency toward boredom.

Spencer Creek Conservation Authority

Shortly after I was elected to the Ancaster Council I became friends with Norman Pearson, who was Director of the Hamilton Wentworth Planning Area Board. Norman was quite a remarkable person. He was English, educated in England, and was a very sophisticated, articulate and principled person. It was Norman who first told me about the Conservation Authorities Act. The Act was passed in 1946 and was roughly modelled on the Tennessee Valley Authority in the United States.

Authorities in Ontario were based on watershed boundaries rather than on political ones. For example, the Grand River Conservation Authority encompassed all the land whose water drained into the Grand River, either directly or through its tributaries. The Conservation Authorities had a wide-ranging mandate for water management, land management, historical site preservation and recreation. Pearson pointed out to me that the Spencer Creek, which has its source in Puslinch Township in the County of Wellington and flows southward through Dundas and eventually into Cootes Paradise, was not organized as a Conservation Authority. In 1958, there were twenty-five or so authorities, but not one for the Spencer Creek.

Although the Spencer Creek watershed was tiny compared to the Grand, for example, I was excited by the possibilities of what could be done if we could organize the Spencer Creek into a Conservation Authority. Norman, as planning director for the county, lobbied the municipalities which were totally or partly within the watershed to get them onside. They were the Townships of Puslinch, where the headwaters of the Spencer originated, Beverly, East and West Flamborough, Ancaster, and the Town of Dundas. The Town of Dundas was the municipality most eager to create the Authority because of years of flooding problems.

Following the procedures required under the Act, the government organized a meeting with the municipality representatives on March 28, 1958, in the old town hall in Greensville. The meeting was chaired by A. H. Richardson who was Director of the Conservation Branch of the Department of Planning and Development. The proposal for creating an authority for the Spencer Creek was universally accepted and two months later on May 6, an Order in Council was passed to officially create the Spencer Creek Authority.

On June 20th, the newly created Spencer Creek Authority held its first meeting. At that meeting, Les Couldrey, who was the mayor of the Town of Dundas, was elected Chairman, and I was elected Vice Chairman. At that point, we had created a conservation authority but, as a start-up, we had no budget and no plans. However, we had been told by the Conservation Branch in Toronto that it would undertake an in-depth study of the Spencer Creek watershed, including a study of its history, its forest and land uses, and make recommendations to the Authority for its consideration. That document took two years to prepare. The Spencer Report which was presented to the Authority around 1960, was and remains the best and most thorough study of the watershed. I would highly recommend it to anyone who is interested in studying the watershed and its history.

The Authority did not wish to remain idle waiting for the report to be prepared. We were aware of some of the proposals that would be made and we took some small steps to begin the implementation of what we knew would be included in the recommendations.

It was during this period I began to realize what local politics meant and how small-minded some local politicians could be. Even as a fledgling authority, with a budget set at around $1000, we began to see arguments arising between municipalities as to what share they should pay. Even amounts of money that were barely pocket change could result in an appeal to the Ontario Municipal Board. In fact, the first budget was $1000 for administration. At that time, of course, we had no staff, owned no land, nor rented any space. We carried on our affairs by meeting at the Collins Hotel in Dundas or at McMaster University. At that time, the Ontario Government subsidized 50% of the cost of Conservation Authority programs.

Although we had no staff, the Conservation Branch assigned a field officer to us whose duties were shared with an adjacent conservation authority. His name was Dave Murray and we could hardly have been more fortunate. He was a highly intelligent and skilled conservationist with all the right instincts. His salary of course was covered by the government. Initially, our Secretary Treasurer was a volunteer by the name of Tom Thomson, a retired school teacher in Dundas. He maintained our minutes and did a great deal of work without any compensation. He eventually wrote a short book called The Spencer Story, which I would recommend to anyone interested in the history of the early days of the Authority. Thomson's role was shortly taken over by John Becker, who was an administrator at McMaster University.

Our First Year

In our first year, we began to look at lands that might be acquired. We considered Beverly Swamp, the Lions Club Camp in Ancaster and the Dundas Public Utilities dam at Crooks Hollow. In those days Conservation Authority projects were called schemes. In order to spend money on any project, it would have to be approved by first the Authority and then by the Conservation Branch. The first scheme adopted by the Authority was the Crooks Hollow / Darnley Mill area in Greensville.

I don't recall at this point how John Becker linked up with us, but I can say that he and I became very good friends and remained so for the balance of his life. While John was our Secretary Treasurer, we rented our first office, which was on Main Street in West Hamilton, more or less across the street from McMaster University. It later became a Chinese restaurant.

John Becker was not only a good administrator, he had a full understanding of the meaning of conservation and good land management. I recall talking to John regarding an idea I had about creating a very substantial conservation area in the Dundas Valley. We knew that the conservation report would contain a recommendation to acquire a couple of hundred acres in the valley; however, I believed the valley was relatively untouched, and as such, was a natural conservation area that needed to be protected from growing urban development. I thought the ideal size should be more like 5 or 6 thousand acres, not the two hundred the report would recommend, but I knew that that would not be a saleable idea to local politicians. I asked Becker to work with me on my idea. We decided about 2000 acres would be politically doable. Becker prepared a large map of the valley showing a proposed conservation area of about 2000 acres. Knowing land prices in those days, I thought it could be acquired for about one million dollars.

    I presented my idea at the next Authority meeting in January 1959. As it happened, Joe Sams, the Reeve of Waterdown was at the meeting because the Watertown Council was considering joining the Authority to include the tiny Grindstone Creek. The creek flowed through Waterdown into Lake Ontario, but as the watershed fell between the Spencer Authority and the adjacent Authority to the East, it was a bit of an orphan. That never happened. When he reported back to his Council about my proposal for a 2,000 acre, one-million-dollar conservation area, they thought my idea was totally insane and decided to have nothing to do with the Spencer Creek Authority.

I Become Chairman

I became Chairman of the Authority in 1964, with John Becker acting as our Secretary Treasurer. We decided we needed a full-time staff person to do various planning tasks for us. John Coates applied for the job and was interviewed by our field officer Dave Murray who sent John to be interviewed by me. I thought he was just fine. And so, he became the very first employee of the Authority and remained in this post for the balance of his career. He was a steadfast member of the staff, engaged in planning and design work. John was also a fisherman par excellence and if I had to guess where he is today it's probably near or on some body of water with a fishing rod in his hand.

Some Acquisitions

As stated, the very first scheme adopted by the fledgling Authority was Crooks Hollow / Darnley Mill in June 1959, a year after the inception of the Authority. Land acquisitions for this area eventually took place and the official opening of the Crooks Hollow Conservation Area occurred on July 9, 1969.

The first land actually purchased by the Authority was 50 acres in the Beverly Swamp in December, 1959. The Beverly Swamp is the largest swamp in Southern Ontario and comprises 2500 acres (928 ha). It provides an extensive natural water reservoir on the Spencer Creek. Over the years the entire swamp has come under Authority ownership.

The Valens scheme was adopted by the Authority in February, 1961. That project was to involve the construction of a dam and the creation of a lake as well as camping facilities. I recall being reluctant about any development at Valens, fearing that it might impede land purchases throughout the watershed. Fortunately, those fears were unfounded as there was no evidence it, in any way, impeded other conservation projects. A number of properties were purchased in the area in 1961 and by 1965 a dam was under construction to create a large lake which was then stocked with bass. As a result, it has become known as a popular bass fishing lake. One of the acquisitions included a fine old farmhouse.

The official opening of the Valens Conservation Area was on June 28, 1968. We needed to find a superintendent for Valens. In the early days of the Authority, every meeting was attended by only one member of the public, and that was Jim Anderson. He was a most affable and capable person who at the time was employed by Westinghouse, one of Hamilton's largest industries. However, his real interest was conservation and so he was our natural choice when it became time to select a superintendent for Valens. He was married to Ruth and they had several children.

Incidentally, Ruth later volunteered to work in my campaign headquarters during the Provincial election of 1971. This was her first "business experience" having spent her adult life as a mother and homemaker. The experience of working in my office revealed talents in Ruth she didn't know she had and she went on to go to University, earn a degree, and become a professional: I do not recall in what field. Jim continued as superintendent, living in the grand old farmhouse into the 80s. The Authority was so lucky to have such a man in its employ.

Valens Conservation Area, partial view of the lake.

The Christie scheme was adopted in November, 1964. This was to be a large project involving the construction of a dam and the creation of Christie Lake. The total acreage of that project was 872 acres (353 ha). The project necessitated the expropriation of a number of properties in the area. The official opening of Christie occurred on June 25, 1974, just after I left the Authority. Christie is one of the most popular conservation areas in the Authority and is perhaps best known for the famous and popular semi-annual Christie Antique and Vintage Show, which occupies ten acres of land at Christie and draws dealers and buyers from across Canada and the United States.

Christie Lake

Because of its proximity to the Niagara Escarpment, the Hamilton region is home to more than one hundred waterfalls and cascades and thirty-two of them are located within the confines of the Hamilton Conservation Authority. A number were acquired during my years with the Authority and the following are a few examples of conservation areas which include beautiful waterfalls.

Tiffany Falls in Ancaster was acquired by the Authority and officially opened as a conservation area on July 12, 1969. It is difficult to judge the beauty of one waterfall over another but Tiffany ranks as one of the most beautiful on the Escarpment. It's a small site and unfortunately does not include much of the surrounding land which is still in private ownership. Tiffany is accessed from a small parking area partway up the escarpment on Wilson Street.

The Devil's Punchbowl Conservation Area opened in 1971. This waterfall, located near the headwaters of the Red Hill Creek, is said to be one of the Niagara Escarpment's most amazing sights. Borers Falls is another very picturesque waterfall located just outside the Town of Dundas. It opened as a conservation area in December 1969.

Tom (middle) Opening of Tiffany Falls Conservation Area, July 1969

Devil's Punch Bowl

The initial development of Fifty Point Conservation Area, located on Lake Ontario in Stoney Creek at the eastern extremity of the Authority, began in the summer of 1970 with the purchase of some 142 acres. It opened to the public in 1984. It totals 80 hectares and includes a marina, restaurant, swimming areas and parkland.

Marina at 50 Point Conservation Area

The site known as Woodend, located near Mineral Springs in the Dundas Valley, was an historic stone farmhouse sitting on a substantial acreage of land. It was owned by George Donald, a long-time Ancaster resident and manufacturer in Hamilton. He had purchased the property for its historic value and in the interests of preserving it. He donated the land to the Authority and the Authority paid a modest price for the house itself. It eventually became the Authority headquarters in 1972, shortly after I left. It might be difficult to find a headquarters for any organization that would be more beautiful than Woodend in its natural setting. As a side note, the house had been owned at one time during the nineteenth century by Ancaster's tax collector who was shot by an unknown assailant on the stairway to the second floor. The crime remains unsolved but the motive may be surmised.

Woodend, Ancaster, Ontario

Borers Falls

Tews Falls

With the exception of Niagara Falls, there may not be any site in southern Ontario as spectacular in its natural beauty as the Spencer Gorge, Tews Falls and Webster's Falls Conservation Area, now known as the Spencer Gorge Wilderness Area. At the inception of the Spencer Creek Conservation Authority in 1958, the only part of this area in public ownership was Webster's Falls and its adjacent park, which was essentially owned and administered by the Town of Dundas. The rest of the land, including Tews Falls, Spencer Gorge and the Dundas Peak were in private ownership as was the land on the westerly side of the gorge. The area of course was well-known to local people and the Ontario Government Conservation Branch recommended the acquisition of the entire area as a conservation project for the Spencer Creek Authority.

It was certainly high on my list of priorities, but in the early days of the Authority there was little financial ability to move forward with such projects. In 1964, we became aware of the availability of what was known as the Tiplady estate. This property was located at the end of Fallsview Road. We had heard there was a plan to build a high-rise apartment building on the site which would've been something of a sacrilege in my opinion. Anyway, we moved forward with the purchase of that property, some 8 acres.

Following that, we continued to acquire the various parcels of land that would be required for a conservation area at this site. That included parcels of the tableland and the gorge on the west side of

Spencer Creek from such owners as Spears (14 acres), Simpson (47 acres), and MacLennan (10 acres).

The east side of the gorge out to the Dundas Peak Overlook was owned by Canada Crushed Stone which theoretically had every right to quarry that area. Standing on the peak one could see the railway station below, the entire town of Dundas, the Dundas Valley and Ancaster beyond, as well as the valley towards Copetown in the West, the City of Hamilton in the East, with Lake Ontario beyond. The views from this site are nothing short of spectacular.

I invited the CEO of Canada Crushed Stone to join me for lunch at the Hamilton Yacht Club. I remember before we sat down to lunch I told him that before lunch was over he was going to be donating their property on the escarpment, including the Dundas peak and the east side of Spencer Gorge, to the Conservation Authority. Corporations could not make land donations and get a tax deduction but they could make a cash donation and then take a deduction for that. So, an arrangement was made whereby we would purchase the land for its fair value and Canada Crushed Stone in turn would donate that amount back to the Conservation Authority. That worked out well and a bronze plaque commemorating this event was erected near the peak. It disappeared shortly thereafter and I suspect that plaque is on someone's grandfather's recreation room wall today. It would be nice if somebody returned it, no questions asked!

However, acquiring Tews Falls and its adjacent lands was not so easy and it turned out that after negotiations to buy the falls and land failed, the Authority was left with no choice but to expropriate the site, which totalled some 32 acres. At the time we were assembling these lands, we were aware of concerns by people who lived on Fallsview Road, which ran adjacent to Webster's Falls and terminated at the west rim of Spencer Gorge. They opposed the project because they anticipated it would draw undesirable traffic to their neighbourhood. Although I sympathized with their concerns, I did not think the alternative, which was to keep the lands in private ownership, was acceptable.

Assembly of the land was mainly completed by the time we had our official opening of the property in September 1967. Normally, official openings are happy occasions with local dignitaries doing such things as cutting ribbons and making nice speeches. It turned out to be not that way at all. The people from Fallsview Road had organized a protest and every property owner on the road had erected a "For Sale" sign on their front lawn and picketed the opening ceremony. I don't know what they hoped to accomplish: stopping the project was not going to happen. But if the purpose was simply to embarrass us, in that regard they succeeded.

One of the speakers at the opening ceremony was Ray Connell, MPP, the local member for that area who lived not far from the site. He made a number of negative remarks about the project and the Authority, pandering to his voter base. He had no useful or helpful suggestions to make to solve whatever issues he had.

Of course, the protesters had legitimate concerns: they were worried about an increase in traffic and certainly that has occurred. In fact, it has caused serious concerns up to the present day, especially on fine summer weekends when too many people and too many cars are crowding the area to see this spectacular sight.

I do not know what the solution to the problem is: as long as there are beautiful natural scenes to be seen people just want to see them. One part of the problem is that there are private residences too close to the site and the other part is that there are too many people wishing to access this area on weekends. Regardless of these present-day issues, the Spencer Gorge / Webster's / Tews area came into existence long before there were people and will still be around long after there are no people left to visit.

Webster's Falls, Greensville Ontario

Tews Falls, Greensville, Ontario

Ice cone at Tews Falls

The Dundas Peak

The Spencer Creek Conservation Authority Becomes the Hamilton Region Conservation Authority

We always knew the Spencer Creek Conservation Authority had to expand to include the City of Hamilton, thereby bringing in its population as a financial base. After all, it was the people in the city who would be the main beneficiaries of the conservation projects. I began a private campaign to convince key people of the Board of Control for the City of Hamilton that it should join the Authority and I spent a lot of time lobbying members of City Council about joining. At one point I asked the Minister responsible for Conservation Authorities to assist in persuading the city that they should join us, but he said we were on our own, and that he would offer no assistance in that regard. Eventually, of course, the city did join and we then became the Hamilton Region Conservation Authority. I became its first Chairman.

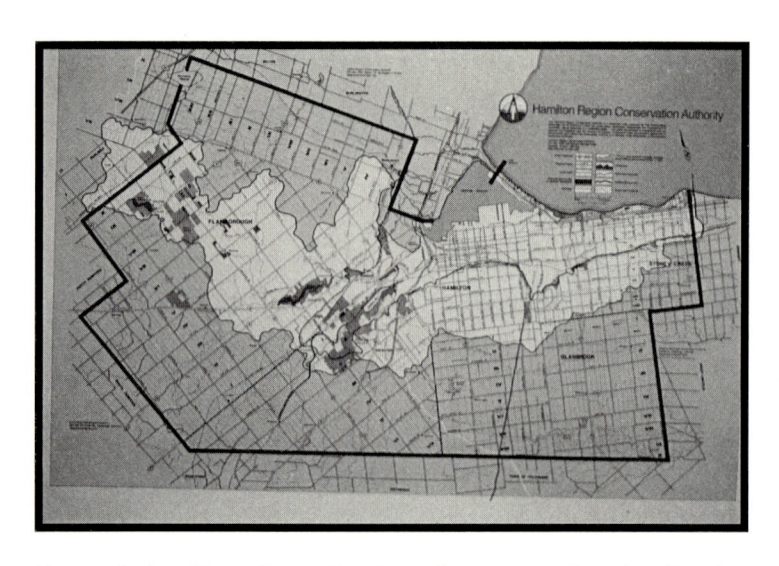

Map of the Hamilton Region Conservation Authority

One of the new members of the Board was City of Hamilton Controller Jack MacDonald, who subsequently became mayor of the city. Over the years, Jack and I came into conflict many times on many issues. He was an interesting person in that he was well-spoken and, in many ways, very likeable. He was certainly able to tell a good story. But he was a strong right-winger and thought it was his duty to oppose just about everything the Conservation Authority wanted to do. As a result, the Board meetings of the Authority became very unpleasant. There was hardly a proposal that MacDonald did not oppose. He seemed to intimidate everybody else and it was left to me to take him on in debate. I remember before going to a Board meeting I would feel almost sick knowing that the rest of the evening was going to be spent in unpleasant debate. I don't know what drove Jack MacDonald or why he seemed determined to quash just about anything that was good for conservation. One of the remarkable things was that after the meeting Jack was always affable and friendly.

Ben Vanderbrug

In 1966, after Hamilton joined the Authority, and we became the Hamilton Region Conservation Authority, our Field Officer Dave Murray was re-assigned to another authority. In his place, the Ministry assigned Ben Vanderbrug to the Authority as its resource manager. Ben was a tall, handsome 28-year-old Dutchman with a beautiful family. Between 1966 and 1970 he was actually employed by the Ministry, but in 1970 he became the General Manager of the Authority. Ben had been educated in the Netherlands and in Canada in tropical agriculture. He and I developed a great working relationship to which I attribute the phenomenal success of the Authority during our years together. Our working relationship became a close personal friendship which continues to this day.

Ben Vanderbrug, former General Manager of the HCA

Lord Bertrand Russell

In 1962 Bertrand Russell, the British philosopher and certainly one of the great philosophers of our time was sent to prison in Brixton in London after his street protests against the use and development of the atom bomb. He was 88 years old at the time. I was shocked that such a great man could be imprisoned essentially for protesting the bomb. The only thing I could think of doing was to write him a letter of support which I did. To my delight and surprise, he responded with a personal letter.

Subsequently McMaster University, of all the universities in the English speaking-world, acquired the Russell papers. It was quite a coup for McMaster. When I learned of this, I contacted the curator of the papers and told him about my correspondence and asked if they would be interested in having it. He said he certainly would as it was the only known connection between Lord Russell and the City of Hamilton. I am quite proud that my correspondence with Lord Russell is part of the Russell papers at McMaster.

I Meet the Face of Evil

During the 60s and 70s, when my children were growing up, we made an annual trip at Spring Break down to the coastal waters of South Carolina or Georgia to camp for ten days or so. During that time period in the United States ghastly things were happening especially after Lyndon Johnson became President. Murders of civil rights workers in the South by the Ku Klux Klan were dominating the news.

We used to like to take back roads coming home from those trips and in the spring of 1965, we were returning through North Carolina when I spotted a sign on the side of the road that said, "KKK Rally Here Tonight". I drove a few miles further down the road and then made a U-turn and started back. I said to Joan, "We are going to the Klan rally." I wanted to see what these evil people looked like. I thought we would be relatively safe. She thought I was a bit nuts but went along with the idea anyway.

There was a motel at the site and I went to the desk to check in. I said to the desk clerk, "I see you're having a bit of a shindig across the road here tonight". "Yes," he said, "do you want to know more about it?" I said, "Sure." He went in the back room and brought out a man he introduced to me as Bob Jones, who was, it turned out, the Grand Dragon of North Carolina. (Interestingly, I recently saw a PBS documentary about him and the Klan in North Carolina.)

Mr. Jones was a bit of a charmer. I told him I wanted to go to the rally and told him who I was, where I lived, and my interest was because I was curious about the Klan. I told him I had heard some very bad things about the Klan but that I wanted to check them out for myself. He seemed to think that was fair but cautioned me not to take photos of anyone at the rally unless I had their permission first. He explained that a number of people who were going to be there were wanted by the FBI.

This was late afternoon but as it grew time for the rally to begin, I went out to the parking area and spotted Mr. Jones talking to a sheriff. I thought it might be wise to confirm my arrangements with Mr. Jones in the presence of a police officer, for what it was worth. When I went to the rally, which was in a large cornfield across the road, it was already underway. I noticed there were perhaps thirty or forty Klansmen dressed in white robes and tall white pointed hats. I also noticed a similar number of what I would call Nazi storm troopers dressed in uniforms that looked like US Army dress uniforms with steel helmets, each carrying what appeared to be a long 5 battery flashlight. I'm sure they were actually intended to be used as weapons.

I had a camera slung around my neck and even though I was as casually dressed as any tourist, I think I stood out like a sore thumb. I might just as well have been wearing a tuxedo and a top hat. I did not blend in with this group at all and I was constantly receiving very suspicious looking glances. I tried to get pictures of some of these "troopers" but this was not so easy to do. Finally, I came up with an idea. I approached one of the young storm troopers and said to him that I thought his uniform was one of the most beautiful I had ever seen. He looked at me and said, "Do ya think so?" and I said, "Of course I do". Then I said, "Do you think it would be possible for me to take a picture of you in that beautiful uniform?" And he agreed.

Some of the Klansmen seemed to soften to my presence and a couple of them posed for my camera. However, most of them continued to watch me with obvious suspicion. There were women and children present as well and even some of the children were outfitted in Klan costumes. I don't know how many people were there, perhaps 100 or 200. It was hard to tell: it was in a cornfield and all the cars were parked somewhere out of sight.

A large flatbed truck served as the stage and soon the speeches began. The first speaker was a man I called The Preacher because he wore a black robe with a sequinned cross on the front. He ranted on about the biblical justification for segregation, i.e., robins mate with robins, cats mate with cats, France is for Frenchmen, America is for Americans, etc. I kept waiting for him to say Canada is for Canadians, but of course he didn't. I learned only about a year ago or so on the PBS program about Bob Jones, that this preacher fellow was in fact an undercover informant for the FBI, although if I had gotten into trouble that night I am sure that he would not have helped me.

A man I called The Cardinal made a similar speech, and named a white local resident, whose address he gave, who had cut the hair of some "nigger" the implication being, that you know where to find him and you know what you should do. It went on and on like this. There was also lots of music like *Onward Christian Soldiers* and other hymns.

Klansmen, North Carolina, 1965

Cross Burning, North Carolina, 1965

At this point, my wife Joan arrived with my three children with a hamburger from the restaurant at our motel. I was just starting into my hamburger when some security guards in their Nazi-like uniforms approached me and said, "Come with us". At this time, Mr. Jones still had not made an appearance. I followed them behind the big truck and a number of them started to grill me about who I was and what I was doing there. I continued to eat my hamburger as I thought it looked cool but I was actually quite scared. When they seem to be getting a little aggressive, I said, "What's wrong with you guys? Bob Jones told me it was OK to be here and to take any pictures I wanted." One of them said, "Oh, Mr. Jones said that?" I said, "Yes" and he apologized and I returned to my place in front of the stage.

There was an area about 40 feet square that was roped off in front of the stage. After more music and more speeches Bob Jones finally appeared. He spotted me at the edge of the roped-off area and immediately strode across the open space in front of the platform and shook my hand. I must say I was never so glad to shake anyone's hand as at that moment. He asked me if I was getting all the pictures I wanted and I told him the floodlight on the stage was a problem. Jones then called The Cardinal over to help me. He took off his red peaked hat and used it to shield my lens while I took pictures. In fact, one of my photos from that night shows a red triangle in one corner, which was part of The Cardinal's hat.

After the speeches, the security guards used their helmets as collection plates and passed through the crowd for donations. It was difficult to know how many people were there, as it was dark. After the collection was over, I decided that since I had poked my nose into just about everything else, I might as well poke my nose into the count too. So, I went behind the stage to where they were to count the money. I counted along with them and as it turns out, when I asked how much they had collected, it came to $34 and some odd cents, which was within a couple of dollars of my count. I asked them how many people were there and they said 5000, a figure, of course, I did not believe. A few hundred might have been more accurate. But whether it was 5000 or 50 people, $34 was hardly an indication of any financial support for the Klan.

After the money was counted, there was to be the burning of the cross. I thought that might be a risky time so I sent Joan and the kids back to the motel and told them to lock the door. The assembled crowd then moved several yards into the cornfield where a wooden cross, about the height of a telephone pole and swaddled in oil-soaked burlap, had been erected. Klansmen bearing flaming torches formed a circle around the cross and the security guards formed another circle around the Klansmen. I recall them singing something. At some point on a signal, the Klansmen tossed their flaming torches into the base of the cross, which erupted into flames. The whole scene was surreal. I took a picture or two, decided it was time to get out of there, and then slipped quietly into the cornfield making my way back to the motel. I checked on Joan and the kids to be sure they were OK and then went into the restaurant. It was full of Klansmen. As I sat having my coffee, I realized everyone in the restaurant was watching me and that I might be in some trouble.

Then I noticed the man I called The Cardinal get up and go out the door to the parking lot and I followed him immediately. I asked if he had any literature on the Klan as I was interested in getting some. He said he did and we went over to his ageing Cadillac. He opened the driver's door and there between the door and the driver's seat I saw a shotgun. He got out several copies of a magazine called "The Fiery Cross" and a poster that said, "Join the KKKK, (the Knights of the Ku Klux Klan) - help fight integration, communism and modernism".

After he gave me this material I went back to the motel room and tried to wake up Joan to tell her we needed to get out of there immediately. She said she was too tired, believe it or not, and went back to sleep. I was afraid the Klansman were going to come through the door, so I sat there most of the night. I removed the film from my camera and hid the exposed roll, reloaded it, and advanced it about 17 frames, but they never came in.

It was beginning to break daylight, so I made my wife and children get up and get into the car right away and off we went. It was a frightening experience and I am not sure why I did it. I probably put myself and my family at some risk but on the other hand the risk was probably low and I wanted to see what was happening in the real world of North Carolina. I have yet to meet another person who has ever been to a Ku Klux Klan rally. We all survived and

I was able to see face-to-face the viciousness of racism in the United States. It may have improved somewhat today but in my opinion the United States is still a racist society.

The Dundas Valley By-Pass

Somewhere around 1967, I became involved with a few other key people who were concerned about quarrying on the Niagara Escarpment, especially in the Halton area. We came together as a task force to have a closer look at the problem and to see if we could come up with recommendations for the Ontario Government with a view to saving it from the destructive ravages of quarry operators. One night, I had attended a meeting of this group in Milton and was on my way home. As I was passing through Waterdown, listening to the radio, I heard a news report which shocked me so much that I pulled the car onto the shoulder of the road to digest what I had heard.

The Minister of Highways for Ontario, the report said, had announced that day the Government was going to build a new four-lane highway from Peters Corners, where several highways converge, all the way to the intersection of Mohawk Road and the yet unfinished Highway 403 in Ancaster. As I sat at the side of the road projecting the route in my mind, the reality of this monstrous proposal fully dawned on me. The highway, to be known as the Dundas By-

Pass, was to slash more or less diagonally across the Dundas Valley. It was to cut through hills, valleys and streams, destroying all in its path. Ironically my own home, I was to later learn, on the Old Dundas Road was on the median strip. It was to pass close to the old Ancaster Mill and tear up the escarpment face as it took out such historic places as the Tamahaac Club. It was to destroy what we know today as the Maplewood property and the Dundas Valley Trail Centre. The highway would destroy the Valley.

As I sat by the side of the road in shock I knew that this highway must never happen and that I must muster all my power to stop it. When I arrived home about midnight I decided to call Bill Gold, despite the hour.

This is a good time to tell you about Bill Gold. He was the Editorial Page editor of the Hamilton Spectator. I had known him only for a short time but from my first meeting with him I was very impressed and took an immediate liking to him. Conservation matters were covered for the Spectator by a very bright and capable young journalist named Peter Calamai who later became Science Editor for the Toronto Star and is now Professor Emeritus of Journalism at Carlton University.

I knew it was important that the Authority had good press and loyal support from the Spectator. So, a few days before the announcement of the By-Pass,

I dreamt up a scheme to take Bill Gold and Peter Calamai on a snowmobile ride through the Dundas Valley or at least part of it to show them what a beautiful and magical place it was, hidden in plain sight on the western doorstep of the city. I asked Ben to find a couple of snowmobiles to rent and have them delivered to my house on Old Dundas Road. Bill and Peter were invited and agreed to come out on one fine cold winter day.

After they arrived and we had fortified ourselves for the forthcoming ride into the wilds of the Dundas Valley we set out; Bill behind me on one snowmobile and Peter behind Ben on the other. Now here's the thing: I had never been on a snowmobile before in my life and as it turns out, neither had Ben. It had all looked so easy when I watched people riding on these wonderful new machines. I had no idea that they needed groomed trails and lots of snow. In the bliss of ignorance, the four of us set out across the field to the Steiner property, which was adjacent to mine.

As we crossed the field all was good and I was inwardly gloating at how clever I was to have dreamt up such a brilliant scheme to show these important people why we needed to acquire a few thousand acres of the Valley. After we got by the fence onto the Steiner land, things got a bit rough. There was a covering of snow but not that much. Since we were now passing through forest, overhanging branches and fallen trees, not to mention large boulders, were everywhere.

But I pressed on, giving my sled as much power as I dared. Boy, was it rough! The machine thrashed and bounced and seemed to me more uncomfortable than I had been led to believe it would be. So, I stopped to see how Bill was doing. He was gone! I had lost him! The very man, the editor I had wanted to impress so he would write nice stuff about us! I looked back and there he was about 200 feet behind me struggling to follow on foot. I don't recall where Ben was at that moment with his important passenger, but we soon got back together and decided they had seen enough and it might be best to repair to my living room for another bit of fortification. By the time they all left, it seemed to me that this was a very happy group.

And so, it was a day or two later, that upon hearing the news of the new expressway and I made the midnight call to my new friend Bill Gold. I would not have been surprised if he had hung up the phone. He had not yet heard the news about the proposed by-pass but immediately asked, "What can I do to help?" I said that it must be stopped and I needed the Hamilton Spectator to help lead the way with articles and editorials, the more the better. Bill and top management at the paper, including publisher Tom Nicols, and editor Gordon Bullock, were true to their word and played a critical role in helping to stop this grossly stupid government mistake.

There was never a formal citizen protest group established to fight this ridiculous proposal but I immediately undertook the role of leading the opposition. The next days found me busy phoning, writing, and haranguing everybody I could find who would listen. I got a call from Tom Cherrington, who was a familiar voice to all Hamiltonians on 900 CHML, asking if I would come on his evening show to talk about the issue. When I arrived at his broadcast studio he said he was not sure the topic would draw much interest so he would tell his audience after about 10 minutes that I had another engagement and then excuse me.

However, even before we went on the air all the lines on the phone were lit up. The people had awakened. I stayed on the show until the very end of the evening and even then, all the lines were still lit up. I was somewhat amazed that so many people were concerned and aroused by the prospect of destroying a valley that most had never actually seen. But this was the 60s and the car was still king and politicians, especially local ones, loved highways and the more the better.

My friend Ann Jones who was the Chairman of the Regional Government thought the Dundas By-Pass was a great idea. I recall her saying, "But Tom, the highway will open up the Dundas Valley so that far more people will be able to see it". To her great credit, years later when the Dundas Valley Conservation Area was a reality, I recall on more than one occasion being in an audience where she was speaking and, after noticing me, would acknowledge my presence and say, "I was wrong about the Dundas Valley By-Pass and Tom Beckett was right". Not many politicians have the integrity and gumption to admit publicly to being wrong.

Those weeks following the government's announcement found me giving all the time and energy I could find into defeating the highway. I was at that time a member of the Conservation Council of Ontario, an umbrella organization comprised of representatives from many different organizations in Ontario. I took my case for preserving the Dundas Valley to the Council and convinced it that the valley was a priceless asset, not just for Hamilton, but for all of Ontario.

The Council agreed to take the case to John Robarts, the Premier of Ontario at the time. I was part of a delegation of three that walked into the Premier's office that day. That was the first time I had met John Robarts. He was an elegant, sophisticated and intelligent man whom I admired greatly, despite my being a Liberal. As we proceeded into his office with George Gomme, the Minister of Highways, and before sitting down, Premier Robarts said to his Minister, "George, is there anyone left in the Province of Ontario who is still in favour of this highway?" I knew at that moment we had won: the highway would not be built. I had hoped the Government would follow up with an announcement to this effect but it never came, even to this day. The Dundas By-Pass just faded away to be forgotten by almost everybody today. To add credence to the old story that every cloud has a silver lining, the threat of the highway provided a huge impetus to the conservation authority's efforts to acquire land, not just in the valley but throughout the watershed.

It is time to recognize John Robarts, not just for killing the highway but for all he did in creating and sustaining a conservation authority movement in Ontario. One of his successors, Mike Harris, did whatever he could to destroy the Conservation Authorities by reducing their subsidies from 50% or more to near zero, but thankfully most have survived, although with a much-reduced means to carry out their collective mandates.

African Lion Safari Opening

I was often invited, as Chairman of the Conservation Authority, to attend public events, most of which were not memorable, except for one. I was invited to attend the official opening of the African Lion Safari near Rockton. Shortly before, I had bought a brand-new Buick Wildcat, which was beautiful, but its beauty ran only skin deep. It had a nasty habit of breaking down unexpectedly. As I was driving through the lions' area at the African Game Safari, my Buick Wildcat decided to quit.

Walking out through a pride of lions did not seem like a viable option so I waited and was rescued by Safari staff in their Zebra-striped Safari wagon. A week or so later a photograph of the rescue appeared in Time Magazine.

More Acquisitions

Meanwhile the acquisitions continued. As an example, a man named Charlie Hill and his wife lived in the Dundas Valley, off Sulphur Springs Road, on a lovely property they had owned for many years. He had retired and had no desire to spend any part of his life anywhere else except there. The acquisition of the Hill property was important, if not essential, to the goals of the Conservation Authority. The solution for acquiring this property was to approach him with the idea that we would purchase the land from him and give back to him and his wife a lease for life on the property. The purchase price would take into account that he was getting a life lease. It was certainly a good outcome for him in that he had a major part of the purchase price of the land in hand and was able to continue living on the property until he and his wife were deceased.

They agreed to our proposal and it was a happy conclusion for both the Hills and the Authority.

In 1968 the Authority became aware that Camp Artaban, which was located in the Dundas Valley and owned by the Niagara Diocese of the Church of England, might be for sale. We contacted the Diocese and arranged a meeting with two Diocese officials and Ben and myself at my house in Ancaster. It was clear they wanted to sell the property to a public body and we agreed upon a price of $30,000. The 25-acre parcel included a large conference hall which the Authority subsequently named the Resource Management Centre and operated it as a school to provide environmental education to Hamilton students. However, when the Board of Education ran into budget constraints the students stopped coming and the Authority had to find another use for the building. It was renamed Maplewood and was rented out for special occasions. It was a great building with a large hall. In fact, this is where an appreciation night was held for me by the Authority when I left it in 1973. The Hall was packed for the occasion and many local notables had a lot of nice things to say about me.

Resource Management Centre, Ancaster Ontario, circa 1970

Tom at the appreciation banquet, 1973

However, Maplewood was underused and costly to maintain and when a proposal was made a few years ago by a private school to lease the property on a long-term basis, the Authority was faced with a difficult decision. Its own staff recommended that rather than dispose of the property by a long-term lease to private interests, the building be demolished and the site returned to nature. The Authority made the correct decision and followed staff advice, which was to tear the building down. I might say this was the last environmental issue in which I involved myself publicly, by lending my support to removing the building from the site and restoring the area to its natural state. I think the Authority displayed a maturity and wisdom in this decision, which both surprised and pleased me.

Adjacent to the Maplewood property was a large parcel of land owned by Monarch Developments. Monarch was a large British development company with its Canadian head office in Toronto. Monarch had intended to develop this land and that would have meant a further extension of housing into the valley from the East to the West, adjacent to the existing Pleasant Valley subdivision. I knew this development had to be stopped and so I decided upon the direct approach. Ben and I made an appointment with the President in Toronto. His name was Thompson, a ruddy-faced Scotsman with a twinkle in his eye.

After Ben and I entered his office, I laid out a map of the Dundas Valley on his desk, showing his property as well as the adjacent properties. I said to him, "Mr. Thompson, before we leave here today you are going to donate a large chunk of Monarch property to the Conservation Authority". I remember he smiled and looked at me and said, "Oh, are we now?" I pointed out a small stream on the map that he would have to bridge in order to carry out their development, and stated that under our dump and fill regulations, he would have to get a permit from us to do it. I said that was unlikely to ever be issued as long as I was there.

It was all very friendly, I must say. But I knew there had to be some kind of a quid pro quo so I suggested to him that a hiking trail in the area be named the Monarch Trail. And that is what happened. So, many of you who are out walking in that area will see trail markers with the monarch butterfly stencilled on the sign post will now know it has nothing to do with butterflies.

During my time with the Authority, I always felt that we were in a race with developers and development. When the property along the west side of Old Dundas / Old Ancaster Road became available, we needed to buy the property and bring it into public ownership or lose it forever. We thought it might be a very difficult acquisition but Ben went to the developer / owner and negotiated a very reasonable price. I don't recall exactly the amount per acre but $1200 seems to stick in my memory. Today there is a parking lot off the road which provides access to those who want to hike the trails in that area.

One of the legacies of the last ice age, some 10,000 to 15,000 years ago, is the phenomenon of peat bogs. In our watershed we have one, the Summit Bog, or as it is sometimes called, the Copetown Bog. I must confess I knew little about peat bogs in those days, and not much more so today.

The Copetown Bog is located just east of Highway 52, south of the hamlet of Copetown. I learned that it was in fact world famous. A well-respected and accomplished biologist, Dr. Norman Radforth, from McMaster University, had been conducting research on the bog for years. He was one of the world's leading experts on bogs, and apparently the Copetown Bog was known throughout the world as a benchmark for scientists.

Summit Muskeg Preserve

"8000 years ago, this depression in the land — a glacial kettle — began to fill with vegetation which fossilized as it died, making a massive deposit of peat. This constitutes "bog" and contains an ancestral record of the present locally unique vegetation which McMaster University in co-operation with the Hamilton Region Authority is investigating."

It came to the attention of the Authority that the owner of the bog, who had always made the site available to researchers, had accepted an offer of purchase from a company that intended to mine the peat moss; the bog was to be destroyed and lost forever to the world of science. In those days, conservation authorities in Ontario had the power of expropriation. It was not something the Authority wished to do, but when the choice was either to expropriate or to see the bog lost, the choice for me and the Board was clear: we had to expropriate. The price to be paid was determined by what the owner had agreed to accept from the peat company.

In accordance with legal requirements, we had Jack Milne, the realtor we employed for almost all our land purchases during my time with the Authority, present the owner with a certified cheque. The owner did not cash the cheque, however, and so far as I know, has never done so. I do not know for certain why he did not, but I have been told that Jack had presented it to him on a Sunday, which had offended his strict religious beliefs. That seems hard to believe and maybe it is not true. I don't know how the Authority accountants have handled this issue but I am sure they must have found a solution by now. Or maybe not.

"Duck Hunting" with Jack Milne

Maybe this is a good time to tell you about Jack. He was with the firm of Chambers and Company. But Jack was more than a hired professional; he was a very dedicated conservationist as well. Jack was the world's greatest punster and an avid outdoor sportsman. It was Jack who introduced me to duck hunting.

One day, he decided to take me duck hunting out on Lake Erie where there were offshore gas wells that had duck blinds constructed at their bases. We had to be in the blind before daylight, so off we went in the middle of the night. We settled into the blind and as it got light, I noticed the lake was frozen out about 150 feet, with open water beyond. I then saw a duck right at the edge of the ice where the water was lapping up and I realized it was frozen to the ice. We watched the duck for quite a while, but neither of us was about to shoot a sitting duck or a duck frozen to the ice. I remember watching it for a long time struggling to get up and away. After a while, I couldn't stand it any longer so I put my shotgun aside and crawled on my hands and knees out on the ice to the duck, and using my pocket knife, I chipped her out of the ice and brought her back to the blind. I said, "Our hunting day is over, Jack, I have to get this bird home as she is obviously in need of care".

When I arrived home, Joan asked me how we did, and I said, "Just fine, I got one," pointing to the hapless mallard under my arm. We put her in the furnace room and nursed her back to health over the next two or three days. Because she seemed okay, I put her in the open creek that ran directly behind our house. I thought I would have a friend for life as she flapped happily around in the water. I then went away for about an hour and came back only to find that my little duck was frozen to the ice again. I chipped her out once more and brought her back into the furnace room but sadly she died a couple of days later. That ended my duck hunting for life. I am just not up to shooting two-legged critters, or four-legged critters for that matter. Sadly, Jack is no longer with us.

Red Hill Creek Valley: The One We Lost

Back in the early 70s, the Hamilton Authority was well on its way to acquiring a large piece of land owned by the City of Hamilton Parks Board in the Red Hill Creek Valley for the sum of one dollar. However, at the last moment apparently, Jack MacDonald, who was a member of the Hamilton Board of Control and also on the Board of the Authority decided that the transfer price should be 1 million dollars, not one dollar.

At that time the City of Hamilton paid 85% of the Authority's budget and the other municipalities paid 15%. That meant the other member municipalities would be paying the City of Hamilton $150,000. I knew then that was not going to happen and that the transfer to the Authority was a dead issue. I have often wondered what would have happened had those lands been transferred to the Authority. Would the Red Hill Creek Valley Highway have been built? I am sure the Conservation Authority would have opposed it but remember the City of Hamilton had the majority of members on the Authority Board, and they may have been instructed by the city to vote in favour of the highway.

The Lincoln Alexander Parkway across the top of Hamilton Mountain was certainly a necessary addition to the road system in the Hamilton area. And certainly, a connection from the east end of the Parkway to the Queen Elizabeth Highway was needed. However, the route chosen by the City, the Red Hill Creek Valley, was in my opinion a fundamental error in planning and development.

So where should the connection have been built? The answer is simple. Let us suppose for a moment that the Red Hill Creek Valley did not exist. The highway would have been built somewhere else. I have always thought the most logical route was Highway 20 which could have been brought up to expressway standards. The city chose the valley because it was cheaper, but they seriously undervalued it as a beautiful open space. In our society we do not place a high enough social value on open spaces as we do for real estate development and highway building. However, the highway has been built, the valley destroyed, and soon there will be few people left to remember what might have been.

Social Planning Council

In the mid 60s, I became involved with the Hamilton and District Social Planning Research Council and was elected to its Board. Harry Penny was its Director at the time. Harry became a close personal friend and continued to be for many years until his death.

He was appointed when the Council was part and parcel of the United Way. The purpose of the Council was to conduct research into community social needs and problems, coordinate work of existing government and voluntary services, and to assist voluntary organizations and government to plan efficient and effective health, welfare and recreational services.

I became Chairman of the Council in 1965, which, incidentally, was a year after I had become Chairman of the Spencer Creek Conservation Authority. During this time, I also became President of the Ontario Association of Urban and Rural Municipalities. Under my leadership, the Social Planning Council decided to incorporate as a separate agency and I became its first president. At the time, it was quite involved with the founding of the School of Social Work at McMaster University. In 1968, I resigned from the Social Planning Council as my run for Parliament was consuming all my time. During all this time, I was also sitting on County Council, running my law practice and raising a family. A busy man with many hats!

I Run for Parliament

Going all the way back to my days at university, some of my closest friends had told me I should go into politics and run for Parliament. I had long ago made up my mind I would never run for Parliament until such time as I was financially independent because I never wanted to be in a position where my financial well-being depended upon my re-election for office. I thought that would mean my independence would be lost and that would be an intolerable situation for me.

In 1968, I was Chairman of the Hamilton Conservation Authority which was moving along with great success and speed in the acquisition of properties and in the opening of new conservation areas. That spring, the Liberal Party of Canada was choosing a new leader. One of the candidates for leadership was Pierre Elliot Trudeau whom I had been watching as a political figure for some time and I had grown to be a great admirer of him. I did not think it likely, however, that the Liberal Party would make him leader. I remember, probably in April 1968, saying to my wife Joan, "You know if Trudeau becomes leader, I think I will run for Parliament," even though I was not by any means financially independent then. I was swept up by his brilliance and his progressive ideas.

Shortly after he became leader of the Liberal Party and then Prime Minister of Canada, he called an election for June 1968. I made a public announcement that I would seek the nomination for the Liberals in the riding of Wentworth where I lived and where I was best known for my activities, particularly in the area of conservation. I did not think I would have any difficulty winning the nomination.

Shortly thereafter, I was approached by three Hamilton Liberal bigwigs, who I know now were sent by John Munro, who was a Cabinet Minister in the Federal Government and Hamilton's leading Liberal, asking if I would consider not running in Wentworth but running instead in Hamilton West, where the candidate for the Conservatives was Lincoln Alexander. I must say, at that time I was new to politics and I think I must have felt flattered that the Liberal Party had asked me to run against such a strong Conservative candidate. Alexander had run once before in Hamilton West and had lost to Liberal Joe Macaluso, who was retiring. Anyway, I was in the hands of the Party and a nomination meeting was eventually called.

However, by that time the campaign was well underway and Hamilton West was already plastered with Lincoln Alexander's election posters. I believe now that the Liberals never expected I would or could win the Riding of Hamilton West against

Alexander. They apparently had taken his election as a foregone conclusion. So, I believe this was their way of putting up a credible candidate against him without the danger that I would actually become a Liberal member and a perceived threat to Munro's position. I think they viewed me as being too independent to be a member of the political flock. They were probably right about that.

Tom and Joan on the campaign trail, 1968

Tom and Pierre Elliot Trudeau, 1968

The Beckett Family, campaign photo, 1968

Anyway, I campaigned continuously for the remaining three weeks. I was handed the campaign organization but I had little or no opportunity to build that organization with my own supporters and friends. I think I surprised them all by the strength of my campaign. When election day finally came, it started to rain in the morning just as the polls opened and heavy rain lasted all day until after they closed. I remember finding out the rain did not affect voter turn-out in the west part of the Riding but it did severely affect the turnout of voters in the north end of Hamilton. The west end was traditionally more Conservative while the north end was solidly Liberal.

So, when the vote was finally in, I had lost the riding by some two or three hundred votes. I had expected to win. If I had followed my own best judgement, I would have sought the nomination in Hamilton Wentworth and I would likely have been victorious there. As it turns out I was the only urban Liberal candidate in all of Ontario to lose in the election. Obviously, had I become a member of Parliament in 1968 my whole life course would have taken a different direction.

As I had expected to win, I must say I felt very depressed following my loss. I think, however, looking back over my life that it was probably just as well. I'm not sure I would've been happy as a backbencher having to tow the party line.

It was after my loss in 1968 that I got to know John Munro and despite his shortcomings, and there were many, I concluded that the man was honest and certainly not the crooked politician so many of his critics portrayed him to be.

Here's an interesting sidelight to the 1968 campaign. In those days I was a smoker and a rather heavy one at that. The day before the actual election I opened a package of Peter Jackson cigarettes and found a gift certificate for $10,000. In those days that was a lot of money. I did not want this to become public knowledge before the election because I did not think it would be helpful to me. I sent a telegram to Imperial Tobacco in Montreal, informing them that I had the certificate and I think somebody at the telegraph office in Hamilton leaked the information because on election day everyone seemed to know that I had won a large sum of money.

Imperial Tobacco said they would organize a party for me at the Royal Connaught Hotel at which they would be presenting me with the check for $10,000. They were very anxious that I invite John Munro who was the Minister of Health at that time. Since it was at the expense of Imperial Tobacco, I invited as many people as I possibly could to the occasion. Following that, Peter Jackson put a large full-page ad in all the dailies across the country with a picture of me, stating, "He lost the election but won $10,000." I was not amused.

I Go to a Rock Concert

Sometime in the summer of 1970, my son John asked to borrow the car to go to a rock concert in Dunmark Park in Ancaster Township. I didn't want him to take the car to the concert so I said I would drive him there.

The road into Dunmark Park angles off Highway 2 over towards Brantford and terminates at the park. As I turned onto the road to drive the several hundred metres to the park entrance, I saw the road was lined on both sides with police officers, mostly OPP, and it was apparent they were searching every person who was entering the park to attend the concert. The people going to the concert were of course all young people, the children and teenagers of our community. I decided to get out of the car and watch the searches taking place. I was quite horrified to see that these young people were being stopped and searched for no apparent reason other than the fact they were going to a rock concert. These were by any definition illegal searches and arrests. If you are stopped and searched by a police officer without your consent that is an arrest and unless there is just cause, it is an unlawful arrest.

I watched young people being taken and placed in front of a police van with flood lights shining against the side of the van where they were fingerprinted and photographed in public view. I could not believe what I was seeing. A radio newsman spotted me and interviewed me and of course I had something to say about what was going on. I saw one girl perhaps about 15 years old in tears after the police had ordered her to dump the contents of her purse, which contained some tampons, on the hood of a police cruiser.

As a result of my public outcry at the scene, I was asked by the Canadian Civil Liberties Union to collect affidavits from young people who had been searched or arrested and many were prepared to provide them. One I can recall was about a young boy who had his bee sting allergy tablets seized and he was charged with illegal possession of drugs. In fact, it turned out they were antihistamines. One told me he had been beaten up in the adjacent field and a girl told me a policeman had pulled her jersey forward and looked down her front. It was to me a scene reminiscent of Nazi storm troopers and I said so on the radio. Of the 10,000 or so young folks who attended the concert there were only about twelve arrests made and to my knowledge not one resulted in a conviction. In fact, considering the numbers of people in attendance it was probably the most law-abiding assembly of people you could ever find.

I later checked with the maintenance people at Ivor Wynne Stadium where the Tiger Cats played and discovered that after every game they collected something in the order of 10 or 11 thousand empty liquor bottles in the stands. Nobody was ever searched going to a Tiger Cat football game. There was obviously a double standard in our community. The reality was that the young people were very law abiding and their parents not so much.

The Canadian Civil Liberties Union then asked me if I would attend as an observer at a rock concert that was to take place a bit later in the summer at a place called Rock Hill, Ontario and observe what was happening and I agreed to do so. I went with my partner and friend Ray Harris. When I got near the site of the rock concert, there was a police roadblock and I stopped. As a police officer stood near my car I could hear his radio announcing that all police officers should be aware of the fact that Beckett had arrived and giving a description of my car and they should be very careful when making any searches in my presence. I looked at the officer and laughed and all he did was shrug his shoulders and smile weakly.

It was pretty much a repeat of what I had seen in Ancaster at the Dunmark rock concert; thousands of people being searched openly and without warrant and without any just cause whatsoever other than the fact that they were young and they were going to a rock concert. I remember driving around the site and coming up on another police roadblock where they had put a wooden gate across the road. I stopped, put down my window and spoke to an OPP sergeant who said the road was closed. I said, "By what authority is the road closed? Do you have a court order?" He just said the road is closed and I said, "Well, I want to go down the road and I want you to open the gate so I can do so". He refused and I said to him, "Well, I'm going to go down the road whether you like it or not". I didn't want to damage the gate and I sure didn't want to damage my car. A stand-off was developing: the officer refused to open the gate. I said, "Well, I'm going to count to 10 and at the end of the count I'm going to drive down the road, gate or no gate". I started counting. My partner Ray, sitting beside me, said, "Tom you're going to get us arrested." Anyway, when I reached about eight in the count the sergeant ordered the gate open. I drove down about 200 metres, turned around and came back through the open gate. I stopped just long enough to say to the sergeant, "I'm just trying to make a point." I don't know what I would have done if he hadn't opened the gate as I was sure not looking to get arrested.

I later learned that around 20,000 young people attended the concert with no serious incidents or criminal offences to speak of. At those two rock concerts the main law breakers were not the kids attending the concerts but the police themselves. I really think that if this happened today there would be a huge lawsuit against the police department. Those were the days of the so-called hippies and there was little sympathy for them. It is ironic that nearly fifty years later the government of this country is now fully engaged in the marketing and sale of marijuana.

Following these two rock concerts about which there was considerable publicity, my family and I were subjected to a certain amount of police harassment. On more than one occasion the police would follow my car if it was being driven by one of my children and sometimes stop them for no good reason to ask where they were going. I remember on one occasion I had gone for a walk around midnight on a mostly deserted Wilson Street in Ancaster. My son was taking his girlfriend home in my car and he stopped on the other side of the street and offered me a ride.

We dropped his girlfriend off and were on our way home when John said there was a police car behind us. I asked his speed and he was well within the limit. Their lights were flashing and we stopped. There were four policemen in the car. I asked the police officer why we were being stopped and he said we had been causing a disturbance by shouting in the street. I knew that was utter nonsense and I wasn't going to succumb to this kind of police intimidation. I told John to drive on, which he did, leaving the police car sitting in the middle of Wilson

Street as we proceeded home. If we had done anything wrong or broken a law I'm sure they would not have allowed us to do that. It was just a continuation of the harassment that my family and I were subjected to by the police following my support of the young people who attended the two rock concerts.

Sudbury Convention 1970

In the fall of 1970, the Conservation Authorities of Ontario held their annual convention in Sudbury. I remember flying into the city and seeing the devastation of the landscape that had been created by the emissions coming from Falconbridge and Inco. It looked like a moonscape and I must say I was angered by the environmental destruction these two companies had caused.

Somehow the local TV station heard that I was prepared to speak publicly about the Falconbridge-Inco environmental damage and I found myself live on the local evening newscast where I condemned the two companies in no uncertain terms on their environmental destruction. Apparently openly criticizing these companies was something people in Sudbury simply dared not do.

I was very disturbed to discover that the convention itself was hosted and partly paid for by Falconbridge and Inco, in what was obviously a corporate attempt to influence those who might have some regulatory control over their actions. Conservation Authorities are public bodies and there is no legitimate reason why private companies should be hosting and paying for their conventions.

One of the people I met there was a young reporter for the Laurentian University newspaper who appeared to be in the bad books of the corporations because of his reporting on the two companies. I discovered they had refused him press credentials for the convention and he was barred from attending any of the functions. When I found this out, I invited him to the final banquet as my guest and he sat at the table with me.

The speaker at the banquet was none other than the Honourable George Kerr, MPP, the Minster responsible for Conservation Authorities. During the course of his speech he startled me by saying, "What conservation authorities need are more chairmen like Tom Beckett". For him to make such a remarkable statement in the circumstances told me he was already under pressure from the corporate sponsors of the convention to get rid of me. Following the convention, I was told by an informant at Dofasco that Dofasco, at the behest of Inco and Falconbridge, was attempting to do just that, but had been told it was not something the Ontario Government could do as I was an appointee of the Township of Ancaster.

Shortly thereafter Inco and Falconbridge built high stacks which alleviated local pollution fairly well but managed to spread it over most of the rest of the Province in the form of acid rain. I'm not sure that was a better outcome.

The Kennedy Story — It Haunts Me Still

I have debated whether I should put this story in my book. However, as this is the only book I am likely to write, I thought perhaps I should include it for what it is worth. First, let me say that I am not a Kennedy conspiracy believer. I have always accepted the Warren Commission findings on the assassination of President Kennedy.

In 1970, I was a sole practitioner with an office in the Terminal Towers in downtown Hamilton and at that time I had one secretary, Mary Roger. One day, a man came to the office and wanted to see me. I was not in, but Mary made an appointment for him to come back at about 1:30. At that time, a man showed up and was ushered into my office. He said his name was Al Fernby. Immediately after he sat down across from me, he wanted my absolute assurance that no matter what he told me, I was not under any circumstance to call the police. He told me that if I called them about this visit he would be dead within the day.

At this point, I wasn't sure what I had in my office. Several times I had to explain to him that I would not be calling the police about anything he was going to tell me unless of course he was planning to commit some crime, in which case I was obliged to call them. I told him that if he had already committed a crime I was bound by legal ethics not to report that information to anyone, including the police.

After receiving what he decided was sufficient assurance from me, the first thing he told me was that his name was not Al Fernby, which did not surprise me. He then proceeded to tell me why he was there. He said he had information with respect to the assassination of President Kennedy that he wanted to sell to the United States Government for $150,000. He assumed that I would want one-third of that amount, so he would net $100,000. At this point, I was quite sure that I had some kind of nut case in my office. I was not exactly sure what I had on my hands so I decided to observe him very carefully. He was a man of middle age and very hard to describe, except that he was an ordinary looking fellow wearing a suit that looked like it had seen better days.

He told me he was a member of the Colombo crime family of New York. When I pointed out to him that I thought he had a French-Canadian accent, he told me he had, in fact, been born in Montreal and had spent part of his life there but had moved to New York. He told me he was on the run at that point, and that he had entered Canada illegally in Vancouver some weeks ago and was making his way across the country. He said he had landed in Hamilton earlier in the day. I asked him where he was staying and he told me he had registered at the YMCA.

He then went on to tell me that there was a connection between the assassination of President Kennedy and his brother Bobby in June 1968. He intimated that both killings had a connection to the Mafia. All of this seemed pretty preposterous to me and I more or less told him so. He was very polite and said he did not expect me to believe anything he was saying — all he wanted me to do was to act as his agent to sell his information to the United States Government.

By this time, I was convinced that I was somehow the victim of some kind of scam but I couldn't see how it was going to play out. I remember telling him that thousands of people had confessed in one way or another to the assassination of the President and I told him he would have to give me some information that only the authorities would know about which would validate his story.

He went on to tell me the name of a United States senator that was involved. The Senator seemed to me to be one of the moderates in the Senate and I did not know what to make of that. It was then I decided to flush him out and see if I could find out what this was all about. I remember pouring a glass of water and handing it to him. He did not take it but said to me "You're trying to get my fingerprints, aren't you?" and I replied that I was. He then told me he had never been arrested and had never been a member of the Armed Forces so there would no record of his fingerprints.

I asked him why he had come to my office and he told me he had consulted the directory downstairs and had seen that I was a sole practitioner with an Anglo-Saxon name and had chosen me somewhat at random. Attempting to find out what his game was, I told him that if we sold the information, I would ask for a 10% down payment, that is $15,000, to be paid into my trust account and that the balance of the money and the $15,000 would not be paid out of my account until such time as the American authorities authorized it.

He said that was fine with him. I told him I had been a candidate for Parliament: I had connections in Ottawa and I would make a call to someone there. He agreed and when I asked him to give me a piece of information that would make his story credible to whomever I spoke to in Washington, he said I could use the name of the Senator.

I told him to come back to my office around five and by that time I would have made the deal for him. At this point, I had no idea how I was going to do that. I asked him if he had any money and he said no, so I reached into my pocket and gave him $15. I told him he was to go back to the YMCA, check out immediately and use the $15 to rent a room at another location. He left.

I immediately put in a call to John Munro at his office in Ottawa, whom I think was Minister of Labour at the time in the Trudeau Government. His secretary said he was in a Cabinet meeting so I asked her to please get him out so I could speak to him. She said that was impossible but I was very insistent. A few minutes later he called me back and after hearing my story, said I should call the police. I explained that that was the one thing I had promised I would not do and said I needed the name of somebody in Washington who I could call about this story. He said he would call me back and he did. He said he had spoken to George McIlraith, who was the Solicitor General, and that at 4 o'clock I was to call a Mr. William Sullivan, who he said was the Deputy Head of the FBI.

At precisely 4 o'clock, I called the FBI in Washington and asked for Mr. Sullivan. I was given his secretary who immediately put me through. I said to him, "Mr. Sullivan, my name is Thomas A. Beckett of Hamilton, Ontario" and he replied with a charming voice, "Now that's an historic name". I asked him if he had received a telephone call from Mr. George

McIlraith, and he said, "No, but I know Mr. McElroy," mispronouncing his name, "He is a very fine gentleman." I then went on describe what had happened in my office with Mr. "Al Fernby". He listened in silence.

When I got to the part about the Senator, I told Mr. Sullivan I was not taping the call and he said, "You should know I'm not taping this call either". I did not believe that then and I still don't. I told him that Fernby had said he had documentary evidence and audio tapes. Mr. Sullivan asked whether they were telephone tapes, "Because as an attorney you would know the evidentiary problems with telephone tapes." I told him Fernby had said some were and some were not. I went on to tell him about the proposal to pay $15,000 into my trust account, not to be paid out until the FBI approved it. Mr. Sullivan said that was no problem and FBI agents would be there in the morning with the cash.

He then asked me for a description of the man and I gave it to him. He asked me if I had felt his hands and I told him I had shaken his hand and determined his hands were soft - that he was not a labourer. By this time, I was absolutely stunned as I had expected to have Mr. Sullivan congratulate me for being a good citizen for reporting this matter, but then go on to explain that the FBI considered the assassination a closed case and was not pursuing any further evidence. Instead, at the end of our conversation, Mr. Sullivan said to me, "Now Mr. Beckett, I am going to ask you to do something that you do not have to do as it may be dangerous". I asked him what that was and he said, "After Mr. Fernby returns to your office, I do not want you to let him out of your sight." I said, "Do you really want me to follow him?" and he said, "I just do not want you to lose him."

After the call ended, I sat in my office trying to fathom what had just happened. What had started out as a normal summer day, had turned into a whirlwind concerning the assassination of a president, a conversation with the Deputy Head of the FBI, and an undertaking to track a man who was of obvious interest to them.

Five o'clock came and went, then 6 o'clock and 7 o'clock, but no Mr. Fernby and so I went home. The next day I was to leave for the cottage but came into the office about 9 o'clock in the morning. Almost immediately my phone rang, and it was a Sergeant Blatchford of the RCMP, who wanted to see me. I told him I was going away and when would he like to see me. He said he was downstairs in the lobby.

Two officers came up to my office. They looked more like accountants than policemen. They said they had received a call from Mr. Sullivan, the Deputy Head of the FBI. I asked if the call was from his office or from Mr. Sullivan himself. They said it was from Mr. Sullivan personally. I asked what instructions he had given them and they said Sullivan had said the matter was to treated with the highest priority. I then repeated the story I had told Mr. Sullivan. I said I was leaving to go the cottage for the weekend and they asked how they could reach me if they needed to. I said the cottage was water access only and that I had no phone there. They then produced a map of Ontario and asked me to point out the cottage location, saying they could get to me by plane if necessary.

The two officers came back to see me the following Monday. They told me Fernby had indeed been registered at the YMCA and that he left at about the time I thought he would have. His trail ended there. The Mounties told me they checked every police database to see whether there was any evidence of this man. They came back to see me several times and continued to keep in contact with me almost daily for some time, asking if I had heard from the man. At some point they told me they expected I would be asked to identify his body as they were sure he had been murdered shortly after he left the YMCA.

The story just ends there. Later, I did send a letter to Ted Kennedy, outlining the story, and he sent a letter back to me saying that the Kennedy family had always accepted the findings of the

Warren Commission and asked for my permission to forward my letter to the FBI. I responded that the FBI already had the story and they could contact me again if they wanted to. I heard nothing further from either Kennedy or the FBI.

Sometime following this incident, I had a suspicion that my office had been entered. I hired a private detective to do a search for any listening devices. He found nothing. The only thing that turned out to be missing from my office was the meagre file containing the few notes that I had on Mr. Fernby and the Kennedy correspondence.

Here's an interesting post script to the story. William Sullivan was forced to resign by J. Edgar Hoover in October 1971. Apparently, Sullivan was no admirer of Hoover. A few years later, he was to testify before a House Committee on Assassinations, especially the Kennedy assassination. One day, Sullivan was at his retirement home in New England and was in the woods behind his home when a hunter with a rifle using a telescopic lens shot and killed him. Mr. Sullivan had apparently told friends earlier that should he die suddenly, it would be by murder. I'm not a Kennedy assassination conspiracy theorist but I must say this story still haunts me. The life of a conservationist was not all waterfalls and butterflies.

More Politics

In 1971, I resigned as Chairman of the Authority because I had become a Liberal candidate for the Provincial Legislature. I had resigned in order to avoid any perception of conflict of interest but I did remain on the Board. My expectation was that I might become Minister of the Environment. In fact, at the request of Robert Nixon, the then leader of the Provincial Liberal Party, I had written the Party's policy paper on the environment.

I lost that election but shortly after I sat down for a drink with my NDP opponent, Gordon Vickert, who was a professor at McMaster University and President of their Party in Ontario. He told me that leading up to the election their Party had predicted that I would win Wentworth North, the Liberals under Nixon would lose, and subsequently I would replace him as Liberal leader. Obviously, they were proven wrong. Being a Liberal leader was not anything I had ever contemplated.

For a long time, the NDP had been pursuing me. Sometime during the 70s their Provincial leader Donald MacDonald paid me a personal visit at my home to try to persuade me to become an NDP candidate. On another occasion, a delegation of prominent Hamilton NDPers came to my office proposing I lead a slate of NDP candidates as a mayoral candidate. When I pointed out my strong

Liberal Party connections, they said it didn't matter and I could maintain my Liberal Party membership if I ran. I was very flattered but declined.

My Television Days

Sometime in the early 70s, I had an idea that what the community needed was a television program that dealt with community affairs in an intelligent way. I proposed to Cable 14 that I would do a weekly interview program in that regard. They liked the idea and gave me a primetime slot in the early evening. The problem was that they provided me with no funds so I was on my own in terms of production.

Now, I knew Stanley Burke through some contacts with the CBC concerning a program called The Air of Death. For those of you who do not remember him, he was the anchor of the National News, the predecessor to Knowlton Nash and later, Peter Mansbridge. So, when I thought about who my first guest on my first television broadcast should be, I thought of Stanley Burke, and he graciously agreed to be a guest on my program. He was an elegant man with a rich voice and was a great asset to the CBC. He was the anchor for the National News for about three years and then retired to go on to do other things. He died in 2016. I continued the show for some months but without production money I found it more than I could handle and so the show died a natural death. It was however, an interesting experience and Cable 14 told me it was their highest rated program.

Dofasco Pollution Control

During the late 60s and in the 70s, I found myself frequently being asked to speak to one group or another as I had developed a reputation as something of an expert on the subject of environmental matters. Of course, I was not an expert but I had been strongly influenced over time by authors such as Rachel Carson and her famous book Silent Spring and Paul Ehrlick writing about overpopulation. I seemed to have the ability to convey these philosophies to an audience. So, I found myself invited to speak here and there. On one occasion I was asked to be a substitute speaker for Farley Mowat. He was supposed to address the forestry graduating class at Laurentian University and had to cancel at the last moment. Being asked to substitute for Farley Mowat seemed like a huge compliment to me.

As my reputation grew, I found I was often the recipient of what otherwise would be inside information from different sources. One day, I got a telephone call from a high-ranking person at Dofasco. He told me I should go down to the foot of Ottawa Street and I would see something that looked like it came from mediaeval China. What he said I had to see was a Dofasco pollution control system and he also told me I would be challenged by a Dofasco security guard when I went there. I remember going down to the site, and as I had been told, I was challenged by the security guard. I told the guard I knew that this was city-owned property because it was the Ottawa Street sewer outfall and he had no right to keep me out.

I then saw a man with an 8-foot pole, on the end of which was attached a bucket with many holes punched in it. He was down at the water's edge scooping up buckets of gun-metal grey sludge that was floating on the water. He would then dump this bucket into two other buckets on the shore that were hanging on a yoke that would fit across his shoulders. When those buckets were full, he would carry this contraption up the slope and dump the contents into a barrel. The man informed me that the barrel would be emptied during the night into a tanker truck. He had no idea where the sludge was then dumped and I was never able to find out. I think the answer would not have been good. When I told my friend Stanley Burke and his producer at CBC about the Dofasco pollution control system they sent a film crew to the site and filmed this "ultra-modern system" that Dofasco used to deal with their sludge. No wonder Dofasco did not want this information made public.

There is a Hole in my Conservation Authority

In 1972, after I had left the Chairmanship of the Authority but while I was still on the Board, Stelco and Dofasco applied to the Authority for a permit to infill an area of Hamilton Bay in front of their properties, about 500 feet wide and 5000 feet long. They claimed they needed this property in order to build anti-pollution structures. I knew the story was not true. I recall going to a meeting attended by several Dofasco and Stelco executives and representatives of the Government where I told them in no uncertain terms the Conservation Authority would refuse to permit the infill of that much of Hamilton Harbour. The previous year the Ontario Water Resources Commission had found that Hamilton Bay was on the verge of becoming septic. The infill proposed by the steel companies would move the south shore all the way to the middle of the original bay and greatly reduce the volume of water in the Bay, likely pushing it to the point of being septic.

But here's what government will do for a big corporate donor. By Order in Council, the Government actually deleted the rectangle 500 feet wide and 5000 feet long in front of the Dofasco and Stelco properties from the jurisdiction of the Hamilton Conservation Authority. Since that time, neither Dofasco nor Stelco has ever infilled the property, and so far as I am aware, the Order in

Council has never been reversed. If you looked at a true map of Hamilton Authority holdings today, you would find a rectangular hole of 500 x 5000 feet in the Bay missing from its jurisdiction. So far as I know this is the only conservation authority in Ontario that has had a section of its interior excised in order to accommodate corporate donor friends. I do not believe this has any significant impact on the Authority today but I mention it in order to show the huge influence of large corporations and big donors on political parties.

I Get Replaced

The only time I have ever been dismissed from anything in my life was from the Conservation Authority to which I had devoted a good part of my adult life. I had incurred the wrath of the Ancaster Council because I dared to speak out against their $10 million sewer system proposal. Now nobody can be opposed to having a sewer system in one's municipality and certainly I was not opposed to it. What I was opposed to was the fact that they had attempted to mislead the public as to the reason the sewers were needed. They said they were necessary because Ancaster was being seriously polluted by sewage. I knew this was not true as the Authority regularly monitored for pollution. The real reason was to accommodate developers so they could move ahead with high density development. Essentially there was nothing wrong with this but it was the deception that I spoke out against. Now Council had every legal right to replace me on the Authority. What I objected to however, was the fact that they didn't have the common decency or courage to deal with my dismissal at an open Council meeting. Instead they chose to do so at a secret midnight meeting, too ashamed and cowardly to do it in the light of day.

Shortly before this, the Township Council had tried to replace me over the same issue. The citizens of Ancaster rose up against my being replaced and over the course of a weekend produced a petition with over 1200 names on it, demanding that Council reverse its position. That time the Council had backed down. This time they were successful.

It's interesting to note that sometime after I left the Authority, a knock came at my door about 9 o'clock one evening. When I answered it, I saw it was a member of the Ancaster Council who had been appointed to the Authority as my replacement. I invited him in but he declined. He said he simply wanted to come and apologize to me personally. He said, "We were told things about you that I now know were not true and I just wanted to apologize." It's truly amazing how vicious small-town politics can be.

The Solid Waste Task Force

In the mid 1970s, the Government of Ontario created what they called the Solid Waste Task Force. From the title one might have assumed it was going to deal with solid waste. However, it was in fact created to look only at the issue of soft drinks sold in non-returnable containers. The Task Force was made up of about ten people and seven of them were representatives of industries that had a vested interest in continuing with the use of the non-return soft drink containers. Three of the appointees were to represent independent agencies such as the Ontario Consumers Association, whose delegate was my then wife Joan, and the Conservation Council of Ontario.

The Conservation Council nominated me as their representative but the government balked at my appointment, for reasons which were obvious to me: they did not want me on the Task Force. They asked the Council to nominate someone else but it held its ground and after several weeks the government finally conceded and allowed my appointment. It was easy to see once I joined the Task Force what the result of its deliberations would be. Of the ten members, seven represented the status quo.

The good thing that came out of the Task Force was that we were provided with researchers who were able to produce some very interesting data:

they found that returnable containers (glass) were less expensive for the consumer and their manufacture consumed far less energy. The only downside for the consumer was one of convenience: instead of throwing the container away, you had to return it for a deposit. Despite these findings the Task Force recommended a continuation of the existing system. Is it any wonder I renamed the Task Force the Total Waste Task Farce?

It is interesting that the subject matter of this whole task force involved soft drinks containers, not some essential product, and it did not in any way propose that the consumption of soft drinks be reduced. I was very discouraged by the fact that the government was unwilling to address such a relatively small environmental problem. I mention this because since that time the problem of throw-away non-alcoholic beverage containers has exploded. The widespread use on non-returnable plastic, particularly for water, has become a huge world-wide environmental problem for our landfills and our oceans.

The Institute of Ecology

After I was dismissed from the Conservation Authority by the Township of Ancaster in 1973, I continued to be very active in the green revolution. It was during this time I was appointed to the

Institute of Ecology. The Institute was created by a number of universities in the Western Hemisphere.

Headquartered in Washington, DC, its research programs were financed by and large by prestigious American organizations such as the Andrew Mellon Foundation and the Ford Foundation. One of its main functions was to study environmental impact statements associated with large projects, as for example, the Garrison Diversion Dam in North Dakota. I was nominated by Dr. Donald Chant, one of the founders of Pollution Probe and a widely respected professor from the Department of Zoology, University of Toronto, to act as the representative from Canada on the Board of the Institute. At the time he said of me:

"I think he's one of Canada's leading citizens on environmental issues. He was an obvious candidate as far as I was concerned. He is aware of the problems, willing to work, and is ready to make considerable sacrifices on behalf of the environment."

When I arrived for my first Board meeting, I discovered the Board of Directors was comprised of twelve individuals, nine of whom were members of the National Academy of Science. The National Academy was a very prestigious organization having only 900 scientists as members, and nine of them were on the Board. I was in very distinguished company. During my time, meetings of the Institute were held all over; in such varied locations as North Dakota, Salt Lake City, Mexico City, Washington, West Virginia, Ottawa, New Orleans and other places that I can no longer recall.

Although it is not entirely clear to me why the Institute decided I would make a good chairman for the organization, it appointed me as such in May, 1975. Unfortunately, I did not get much of an opportunity to play a significant role as chairman as in May of that year I suffered a heart attack and as a result had to resign my position with the Institute. For reasons that I don't know, the Institute no longer exists.

Heart Attack!

As heart attacks go, the heart attack that ended my days with the Institute of Ecology was a fairly minor one. I had been experiencing some obvious cardiac symptoms and decided that I should go to the hospital. As I lay in the emergency department all wired up, I suddenly thought about Carol Horncastle. Carol was my client and I remembered I was to appear with her in Family Court the next morning. She had a very violent boyfriend that I considered to be dangerous and a threat to her life. I had to call someone in my office to make sure that somebody was there with her at the Court and to make sure she was safe.

I asked the nurse in the ER for a telephone and she explained to me that it was not possible for patients to make a telephone call from the emergency department. I explained the situation and she still was unable or unwilling to provide me with the telephone. I asked to see the head of the hospital and when he appeared I explained my problem. He agreed that I needed a telephone and had one brought to me. I called my partner and explained the situation and he assured me someone would be in Court with her the next morning.

From the ER, I was moved to another area in the hospital where I was to be monitored. The next morning I awoke in the dark to find myself surrounded by people in white coats. It was of course the cardiologist, along with a group of medical students. After the usual kind of doctor questions I was told I had not had a heart attack and I would be discharged later that morning. I got up and got dressed and was ready to leave the hospital as soon as I was cleared. At that point, I noticed a cleaning lady in my room mopping the floor and I said to her, "Well, I am going home today". She stopped mopping and looked at me and with a very heavy Eastern European accent said, "No meester, you no go home from here. You die maybe, you go upstairs maybe, but you no go home". I told the cleaning lady that the doctors had said I could go home today. She stopped mopping again and said with even more emphasis, "No meester, you no go home, you die maybe, you go upstairs maybe, but you no go home".

"What did the cleaning lady know?" I thought. Shortly after that, the nurse came in and told me I was to get back in bed immediately. My blood tests were back and had shown that I had, in fact, had a heart attack, and so, as the cleaning lady had predicted, I went "upstairs". After I arrived on the ward, I was visited by the cardiologist who told me I had had my last cigarette and that I must never smoke again. Shortly after the doctor's visit, a candy striper appeared in my room pushing a cart full of goodies, offering not just candy bars but various brands of cigarettes for sale. I told the nurse at the station immediately across from my room that I thought it was very strange they should be selling cigarettes to heart patients in the hospital.

She asked if I wanted to do something about this and I said yes, so she asked if I would talk to Dr. George Lewis who a professor of Anatomy at McMaster Medical School. Dr. Lewis was well known in Ontario as a ferocious opponent of smoking. He came to visit me and asked if I would write a letter to the hospital. I said I would do so. As a result of my letter, the sale of cigarettes to patients at the hospital was stopped. It took a few more years but smoking was finally prohibited anywhere in the environs of the hospital.

While these events were happening at the hospital Carol Horncastle appeared in court, which was on

James Street south of that time, with Scott Henderson, an associate of mine. It was only to set a date for a hearing and took only a few minutes. Scott then walked Carol up the street to the corner of Main and James and saw her safely onto a bus heading out to East Hamilton.

The boyfriend apparently followed the bus and when she got off, he snatched her from the sidewalk into his car, and drove her up to the east mountain to a deserted old dirt trail called Nebo Road. They sat there for an hour and a half and smoked a package of cigarettes. At that point she said, if you're going to do it, do it, whereupon he produced a new pair of nylon stockings he had purchased for this purpose and strangled her to death. He then placed her body at the side of the road and covered it with a blanket which he had also brought along for the purpose of keeping the flies off her. He then left the murder scene, met with his brother, and went to McDonald's for a big Mac. The reason we know these details is that this was his own account of the murder given in his confession. As I lay in my hospital bed upstairs on the fourth floor I knew nothing of the events that followed Carol's appearance in court and her subsequent tragic and violent death.

The Great Guatemalan Earthquake

In February 1975, I was in New Orleans to attend a meeting of the Institute of Ecology. I had never been to New Orleans and I thought it was a pretty neat place. After the meeting, I called my friend and law partner Ray Harris and told him he should come down and join me and see New Orleans, and so he and his wife did just that. We had a lovely time and did all the usual things; the jazz clubs etcetera, etcetera.

At some point, we discovered you could easily fly from there to Merida, Mexico, so on the spur of the moment, we did so. Merida is known as the "White City" and is in the western part of the Yucatán. It was lovely place where we found a very comfortable hotel. The first night that we were in the hotel, we were in the bar, where we noticed a woman sitting across the way. After a while, she asked if she could join us. I guess she was a little lonely. I soon found out she was a lawyer from Chicago. I said I was corresponding with a lawyer in the United States that happened to be a Chicago lawyer having to do with the Sears estate. Believe it or not it turned out that this was the very person I was corresponding with! What a small world!

My client was related to Sears' wife and both were members of the Mohawk Nation. I had been retained as a lawyer previously by an organization in Pickering called The Group Against Garbage (GAG), of which my client was a member, to fight a huge landfill site that was being proposed by the City of Toronto. Anyway, it was all an interesting coincidence that I should meet in a bar in Mexico the very lawyer that I was dealing with in Chicago.

Ray and I toured the Yucatan in a rented Volkswagen van and visited several Mayan sites, including Talum, Ushmal and Chichen itza. We were staying at the Hacienda Chichen itza on the 25th of February when for some reason we found ourselves, along with the other guests, awake and out in the courtyard at 3:20 in the morning. No one seemed to know why. It was later in the day we learned that at this very time the great Guatemalan earthquake struck. This earthquake killed more than 20,000 people and injured ten times that number and caused massive damage. It was a disaster on a colossal scale.

Now as it happened, two years later I was in Guatemala visiting my best friend Bill Harris whom I had first met when he was manager of Building Products in Hamilton. He eventually became the CEO of Kruger Pulp and Paper, Canada's largest exporter of pulp and paper. Bill was a good environmentalist and a lover of the outdoors. After he ended his career as an industrialist, he bought some plantations in Guatemala, moved there with his wife Ann and became the country's largest exporter of tropical plants.

Bill survived the earthquake as did his family and subsequently he became heavily engaged in the

Canadian Government relief effort. A little over two years after the earthquake I decided to go down and visit Bill and his wife Ann. This was another interesting trip to Central America where I had the opportunity to visit several more ancient Mayan sites, including Copan, across the border in Honduras, and Lake Atiklan in Guatemala.

In one of the villages in Guatemala that we visited, San Andres Itzapa, the first thing I noticed was that the main street was called Republica de Canada. Bill explained to us that this village had been almost totally obliterated by the earthquake and that the wooden houses we now saw were made of plywood flown there by a Canadian Air Force Hercules aircraft. It was a strange sight to see these plywood structures where you were accustomed to seeing adobe houses. In Guatemala, the poorest members of society lived in thatched roofed houses, the walls of which were made of vertical poles, plastered over and painted white. The people slightly up the economic ladder lived in similar buildings but the walls were made of adobe. When the earthquake struck the pole buildings merely shook but the adobe buildings collapsed, dumping heavy bricks on their sleeping occupants, and causing thousands of deaths and injuries.

Among the buildings that came down was a large Catholic church. It was just a pile of rubble. Beside the church was a strange looking building that was built of some reddish coloured brick and was completely undamaged. It seemed to be a temple dedicated to the worship of the old gods. When the Spanish conquered Central and South America they brought Christianity with them. Christianity did not displace the religions of the Mayans and others; Christ was just added as another deity to their existing gods and beliefs. It is not uncommon even up to the present time for locals to get married at the altar in the Catholic Church and then step outside and have a second ceremony in the tradition of their ancient beliefs.

Looking at the condition of these two buildings, it was understandable which god the locals thought was the more powerful one. Anyway, we entered this building and I saw the strangest sight I have ever seen in my life. It was almost jet-black inside. The ceiling, which may have been white at one time was totally black, caused by many years of burning candles. As we grew accustomed to the dark, we saw there was a stage at the far end of the room and on the stage was an arm chair. Sitting in the chair was a life-sized effigy dressed completely in the uniform of an RCAF officer — everything from shoes to cap. Local people were placing offerings at his feet, either a small bottle of liquor which I think they called quetzalteca or little offerings of cigarettes and food.

I remember watching this and thinking I dare not raise my camera to take a flash picture as I knew I was witnessing something that was of religious significance to the locals and I thought it would be insensitive to these people who seemed to be treating the effigy as some kind of deity. Bill explained to us that after the earthquake the Canadian Government provided very extensive aid, much of which arrived in Canadian Air Force transport aircraft. Having this aid arrive by airplane must have seemed like something sent by the gods.

I have since learned that effigies known as either Maximón or San Simon, exist in a number of Mayan villages and towns in the highlands of Guatemala. Apparently, he is based on a pre-Columbian Mayan god, blended with influences from Spanish Catholicism. Legend has it that he was an elder who was reincarnated to protect his people. By the end of the 19th century, a man believed to be another reincarnation, rose up to protect his people from a corrupt governor. This man was known to be a heavy smoker and drinker and after his death effigies to him were made and his image was honoured with these sacrifices. The effigies, often carved from wood, are still found in shrines, usually in houses, and accompanied the year round by attendants who care for him and look after the money, tobacco, alcohol, candles and other offerings which are left by worshippers who wish to gain his favour in exchange for good health, good crops, marriage counselling and other requests.

Depending on the particular town or village he can be found wearing a wide brimmed hat and dressed in both traditional Mayan clothes and in modern garments, such as a suit and tie, and draped with many colourful scarves, or alternatively, more casual attire and dark sunglasses and a bandana. Obviously, the effigy I saw in 1977 dressed in the uniform of an RCAF officer was a tribute to the reconstruction aid that Canada provided and was delivered to the site by the RCAF. I would not expect the effigy to be dressed that way today. It's all quite mysterious and fascinating. Maximón is one of the present-day reverberations of the great Mayan civilization that existed more than a millennium ago.

An Effigy Today

Guatemala was in many ways a very violent country and I experienced it more than once. I used to plead with my friend Bill to get out of there while he still could, although he planned to move eventually to New England after retirement, he stayed in Guatemala a little too long. He was assassinated by some Guatemalan criminals who were attempting to extort some $7500 from him. On the day of his murder, he had driven from Guatemala City to one of his plantations on the Pacific side of the country. The threat was out there and his wife had urged him to take a guard with him or hire an armoured car service which, if you can imagine, was readily available for such journeys in that country. Other than carrying his own weapon, he decided he would not yield to them in any way. They shot him to death in front of his home, in front of his wife and neighbours. When trying to get his body released from the hospital for burial the doctor demanded a bribe of several thousand dollars in order to do so. His wife Ann had to retain a lawyer to negotiate the cost of the bribe down to a reasonable amount. Bill is buried in Guatemala City. I miss him still.

Such was the life for people in Guatemala. I am not sure it is much better today.

Bill Harris and Tom

Meralee

By 1980, my second marriage had come to an end and I was again a bachelor. My nephew Bill was a travel agent and he suggested I take a cruise and arranged one on a German cruise ship called La Bohème. I had this image in my mind that I was going to meet all these beautiful young unattached American women on the cruise. As I sat in the departure lobby in Fort Lauderdale I was eyeing the crowd, hoping to see all these beautiful young ladies, but unfortunately everyone looked like they were members the bowling club from Omaha, all dressed in polyester and plaid. I saw only one pretty girl and after she went up the gangplank onto the ship she was swept away by the young German crew and I didn't see her again until she departed the ship at the end of the cruise.

The interesting thing about the cruise is that no sooner had we cleared the harbour in Fort Lauderdale when an announcement came over the loudspeaker advising we were heading into rough seas and that seasick pills were available in the ship's dispensary. The seas were huge and I remember waves breaking over the bow of the ship and hitting with great force on the glass in the dining room. People began to get seasick and retreat to their cabins. For some reason I didn't get seasick and continued to enjoy myself observing the other passengers on board. My table companions in the dining room were some of those "bowlers" from Omaha and I swear they were the most boring people I have ever encountered. There was however, one woman on the ship that I found to be extremely fascinating. She was quite an old lady who was dripping with gold jewellery, around her neck and on her wrists and ears, and I quickly dubbed her Mrs. Gold. Every time I saw Mrs. Gold she was talking: talk talk talk talk talk talk! She never stopped talking! I began to find that in itself quite fascinating and would watch her as she continued her endless blabber.

The seas really never calmed. One of the crew members told me that in all the years he sailed the Caribbean this was the roughest seas he had ever encountered. Lucky me. They couldn't even keep any water in the swimming pool. On the final evening of the cruise they held a big banquet in the dining room although it was fairly lightly attended. Mrs. Gold was at a nearby table with six dinner companions continuing her non-stop talking all through dinner. Dessert was the traditional flaming Alaska. Just as Mrs. Gold and her companions began to eat their dessert, she chose that moment to be sick. The chattering abruptly stopped and she projectile vomited, not missing a single one of her companions around the table. I have to say it was one of the funniest scenes I have ever seen in my life. Of course, waiters came running with cloths and started clearing off the table and wiping off her companions. No sooner she had stopped vomiting then the talking began again. I don't remember seeing her again after that dinner but I'm sure wherever she is today she is still talking.

When I returned from the cruise I had a conversation with my daughter Mary-Jo. She was working at the medical centre at McMaster University and told me she had met a really nice person there by the name of Meralee and had asked her if she was interested in meeting her father. Meralee said she was and so I called her. I told her all about my cruise to the Caribbean and about Mrs. Gold. Apparently, she thought I was pretty funny and decided she would accept my invitation to go to dinner a few days later. I remember walking up to the door of her house and being greeted by three curious young boys and an out-of-control dog.

Now, any sensible person would take a blind date to a local restaurant so that if things did not go well the trip home would be short. However, that is not what I did. I took her to dinner at the Alton Inn near Orangeville, about an hour's drive away. Fortunately, we seemed to hit it off on that first date and shortly after we became an item and have been so for the past 37 or so years. She had just turned 41 when we met and I was 55. I thank my daughter Mary Jo for all of this because it were not for Meralee I'm not too sure where I'd be right now.

Tom and Meralee's marriage, December 13 1986

I Become a Judge

Being an environmentalist and a foot soldier in the green revolution does not pay the bills or provide a pension. Late in the 1970s, I became concerned about my financial future and let it be known that I would accept an appointment to the Bench. Although candidates for judicial appointments must be approved by the Canadian Bar Association, the fact is appointments are made by the government of the day. I had twice been a candidate for the Liberal Party and had served in other ways, so I certainly met the political qualifications. For the next few years, I kept my head down and tried to blend in as best I could with the cast of potential judicial appointees.

In June 1984, I received a telephone call from Mark McGuigan, Canada's Minister of Justice, to tell me that I was now a judge of the District Court of Ontario and that I would be assigned to the Unified Family Court in Hamilton. With that phone call, my financial security was assured for the balance of my life. During my tenure the District Court of Ontario and the High Court of Ontario merged to become the Superior Court of Ontario and I therefore became a Superior Court Judge.

Tom and Meralee, Tom's appointment to the bench, 1984

During my years as a judge on the Bench, I found every day in court to be an interesting one. Early in my judicial career I was assigned a case that proved to become notorious. It involved an application by the Children's Aid Society of Hamilton to make two little girls wards of the Crown. There were lurid allegations apparently made by the children of Satanic rituals, murder, dismemberment, cannibalism, and the digging up of dead bodies. The case dragged on for over 150 days in court over the span of about a year and a half.

During the trial the mother of the children gave birth to her third child and that was the cause of some of the delay. However, it became apparent to me the lawyers on both sides of this case were demonstrating the lesson Dr. Fox had taught me back in 1948: only in this case they chose the difficult and hazardous course instead of the simple and direct way. At the end of the long trial, I found no evidence that the bizarre allegations of Satanism actually occurred.

I did find however, that the children had been sexually abused by their caregivers and therefore made them wards of the Crown.

Every day during this long trail, there were a number of reporters present in the courtroom from such media outlets as the Toronto Star, the Globe and Mail, The Hamilton Spectator, the CBC News and others from time to time. One of the reporters who covered the trial faithfully every day was Kevin Marron, who was with the Globe. In fact, at the end of the trial he wrote a book called Ritual Abuse which is a fairly accurate account of the whole trial. There was another book written about the trial by an author who claimed he had been there every day but was in fact there for less than half of one day. Where he got his facts from I do not know. I have not bothered to read his book.

During the course of the trial there were a number of bizarre events and I do not intend relate all of them but one was of particular interest to me. At some point the senior judge for the County, Judge Gordon Sullivan, came to me and told me there had been a threat made on my life and asked me if I wish to carry a gun. I laughed off the suggestion and thought it was rather silly.

However, shortly thereafter, I received a visit in my home in Etobicoke from two Metro Toronto detectives. They told me they had received information from a psychiatrist who was not related to the case but had as his patient the father of the children and who had apparently expressed to the doctor a threat to shoot the trial judge. The officers asked me if I wanted a police escort back-and-forth to court. I said no, all I wanted was a description of the man's vehicle and license plate number so that if I spotted him I would be able to act appropriately. They gave me that information and I kept an eye out in my rear-view mirror for a time. The trouble was that the vehicle description they gave me and the license plate number belonged to another vehicle this man owned, not the one he was likely to be in. So much for security!

Behind the scenes during the trial there was apparently some kind of war going on between the Children's Aid Society and the police. The lead social worker on the case for whom I had a great deal of respect, claimed her own apartment had been entered and surreptitiously searched by the police. I have no way of knowing whether that actually happened but I had been told that the police had searched the home of the father in the case without a warrant and found firearms. I was disturbed by the fact the police were making warrantless unauthorized entries into peoples' private homes to secure intelligence. Some of you may think it's OK for the police to do such things. After all they were acting in this case to protect the life of a trial judge. However, I do not view it that way. We are a nation of laws and under those laws police cannot make surreptitious entry into private homes no matter how noble they may think their actions are. Once this happens it is indeed a slippery slope.

Young Offenders

For a number of years, in Hamilton young offenders under the age of sixteen were tried in the Unified Family Court. A great many of these youngsters appeared before me, mostly charged with minor crimes. It was necessary, from time to time, to sentence them to open or to secure custody depending on the offence. I thought it prudent to pay a visit to some of these custodial facilities to see what sort of places I was actually sending these kids. I arranged to go to a secure facility in Simcoe, Ontario. As I approached institution it looked like a large high school except it was surrounded by a high security fence.

The superintendent showed me around, but she was only showing me the facilities rather than the actual inmates themselves. She seemed reluctant that I should actually talk to the boys. I said I wanted to see the boys so she took me into a common room where there were a number of boys sitting around, many smoking and playing cards. As I looked out the window I could see it was a fine sunny day and I noticed a large sports field with a running track.

I asked a couple of the boys why they weren't outside on the field on such a lovely day. One replied that in order to do that you had to get a TAP, a temporary absence pass, which he explained you could only get by written application which took about four days to process. I said, "You mean you have to apply in writing days in advance before you want to go out and kick the soccer ball around for a bit?", and he said, "That's right". This did not seem logical or believable to me so I drifted off and started talking to some of the other boys and they gave me the same story. I asked one of them how long it had been since he was outside and he said four months.

I went to one of the custodians and said these kids are telling me they need a TAP to go outside to play on the soccer field. And he confirmed what the kids were saying was true. I could not believe this as even the most hardened criminals in the most secure penitentiaries got their time every day in the exercise yard.

Sometime after that my secretary said that some youth at an open custody facility wanted to see a judge from our court. I volunteered. The facility was an ordinary looking bungalow in the east end of Hamilton that housed six boys and their house parents. As I approached the front door I noticed that the walkway was snow-covered. I wondered why these young fellows hadn't shovelled the walk. After I entered, I was invited to sit down at the kitchen table with the six boys, one of whom I had sent there. The first thing I asked was why they hadn't shovelled the walkway. They said, "Oh we can't do that because we need a TAP to go outside". By this time, I knew what a TAP was. I said, "You mean to say you can't shovel the walk without getting a TAP?" and they said that's right. I asked if they could go in the back yard and they said again, not without a TAP. One of the boys said to me "Do you know what the hardest part of living here is?" He said it was the unlocked door. I understood him completely. Most of these boys were in custody because they had grown up in chaotic and undisciplined circumstances. How could we expect them not to take advantage of an open door once in a while? But I now understood for the first time why my youth court docket saw so many charges of "escape lawful custody".

Another thing I saw in youth court was the jailing of kids for truancy. When I said publicly that children were being incarcerated for truancy, the school board was very upset and denied it vehemently. Of course, they were technically right: children were not being jailed for truancy. What would happen was they would be brought into court and the judge would make an order that they must attend school? The next time they did not attend they would not be charged with truancy but with a violation of the court order and that could land them in custody. It was a two-step affair: instead of addressing the reason the young person was not going to school it was thought an order to do so was the solution. It was not.

As a youth court judge, I came to realize that if you're going to commit a crime in this country then you better do it as an adult and not as a young offender. The rights and privileges of young people were pretty much ignored by police and other authorities and I did not think this was the way young people should be treated in our judicial system.

That reminds me of a time I was walking through the Jackson Square mall in downtown Hamilton when I saw a fairly large group of young kids standing about. As I approached them, one of them whom I recognized came forward and shook my hand. He then turned his friends and said, "I want you to meet a good judge." Strange as it may seem that made me feel very proud because I recognized that this young fellow who had appeared before me at one time, respected me and if he respected me that was a step towards respecting the judicial system.

Youth crime and poverty went hand in hand. A study was done by the Social Planning Council that showed the poorest neighbourhoods produce the highest rate of crime, especially among young people. I remember saying once that in all my time in youth court there was only one accused person that I felt might truly be a danger to society. He was the son of a wealthy person in Burlington. All the rest of the kids that appeared before me were what I called little cowboys or cowgirls, most of whom didn't really pose any real threat to anyone.

Part 3

After Public Life

Cottage Life

If you have not already guessed, being at the cottage has been a major part of my life. I already told you about the cottage my father built on Lake Nosbonsing in 1949 which later burned to the ground in a spectacular fire. In those early days at the Nosbonsing cottage, there was no electricity; light was provided by propane lamps. There was no road to the cottage; you could only get to it by water. There was no refrigerator; we had an icebox and to fill it we had to cross the lake by boat to dig out huge blocks of ice from the ice house at Big Moose Camp. After the fire, the cottage was rebuilt and became a place where several generations of our family and their friends gathered regularly in the summer months. By that time, we had a road and electricity. Joan's mother and dad were frequent visitors as was her sister Constance and her husband Laurie and their four children. We were able to spend a lot of time with my dad and mother there. Contrary to many husbands and fathers who were weekend golfers and consequently saw little of their families on weekends, my life was opposite of that: weekends were for my family.

During the winter months we were skiers. I was one of the early members of the Holimont ski club in Ellicottville, New York, south of Buffalo, and every winter weekend when there was snow, the family would head down to ski. We rented the second and third floor of a beautiful old Victorian home in Salamanca, a small town about ten miles from the ski hill, which was owned by the widow of the local doctor. Her name was Florence Stall and she became like a member of our family over the years that we stayed there. While I no longer ski, I have many wonderful memories of our time at Holimont.

My mother passed away in 1967 and my father in 1970. We sold the Nosbonsing cottage and the proceeds were divided between my brother John, my brother Bill and myself. With my share I bought a cottage on Baptiste Lake in 1974 and it became the new hub for family life. However, it was a water access, summer only cottage and as the family grew with the addition of my three stepsons, sons-in-laws and daughters-in-laws and grandchildren, we needed to look for something larger to accommodate everybody. We concentrated our search on Lake of Bays where I had fond memories of visiting as a teenager. We found a lovely lot on the lake where in 1987 we built our present cottage and where we spend our summers to this day. Over the years, our cottage has been a gathering place for family and friends alike.

It was there on a very cold and snowy Christmas Eve morning in 1989 that I suffered a serious heart attack. Meralee and I were there alone waiting for her boys to arrive that day to spend Christmas at the cottage with us. I remember we waited anxiously for what seemed like a very long time for the ambulance to come from Huntsville. It turned out they had gone into the ditch while trying to get down our cottage road in all the snow. I was suffering all the typical symptoms of a heart attack and when I was in the ambulance I could hear the attendant relaying my vital signs to the hospital in Huntsville and they didn't sound very good. I asked him, "Am I going to make it to the hospital?" and he replied, "I have never lost anyone in this ambulance and I am not going to lose you".

Those were magic words to me and I felt like I had been given a guarantee that I was indeed going to make it. I'll never forget that fellow: he was a big Aussie with a black beard. When I got to the hospital, they moved me from the ambulance gurney to the hospital gurney, which promptly collapsed and dumped me on the floor. My cardiologist later told me that if the heart attack didn't kill me, falling on the floor in the ER probably should have. I was kept in the hospital for a week and it ended up that the whole family came to stay at the cottage to see me, including my brother John and a couple of his boys. It was quite a time. They must have been stacked like cordwood in there! I then spent the next six weeks recuperating at home before returning to work at the court.

The cottage lifestyle seems to have passed down to my three children. When we first built the cottage on Lake of Bays we added a wing to accommodate John and his young family. But as their family grew they needed more room so they built a beautiful place on Tobin Island on Lake Rousseau . Elizabeth and her husband Ron had cottages on Lake Muskoka which they have since sold and bought some beautiful farmland only a short drive from their country home near Stouffville.

Mary-Jo and her husband Kevin combined home and cottage life by buying a home in Grey County on 70 acres of managed forest containing streams and a spring-fed pond, which is cold enough the freeze the balls off the proverbial brass monkey. We continue to see Meralee's boys, Mark and Jeremy, frequently at the cottage; Rob not so much as he lives in paradise, on the west coast of Vancouver Island.

Retirement

I served on the Court from the time of my appointment until my mandatory retirement in 2000 at the age of 75. After serving my last day in Court, I took off my gown, put my personal things in my briefcase, walked out of my office down the corridor to the elevator, went down the elevator and out to my car. By the time I had reached my car I had, I think, fully adjusted to retirement and I never went back, not even so much as for a visit.

From 1984, when I was appointed to the Bench until my mandatory retirement on my birthday on

December 23, 2000, I was unable to participate in any public affairs because judges must always remain impartial. I did however become interested in the appearance of the public highways in Ontario. For most of the time, I was commuting between Etobicoke and my court in Hamilton and I became increasingly annoyed and upset about the ugly appearance of the Queen Elizabeth Highway. When the QEW first opened in the 30s it was a beautiful highway with a wide grassy median in the centre, ornate lighting, and attractive landscaping, but its appearance had deteriorated badly over time.

I was aware of many highway beautification projects in the US and, after doing some research, I discovered the existence of what is now called the Ladybird Johnson Wildflower Center that had been founded and headed by Lady Bird Johnson and the famous American actress Helen Hayes. I corresponded with Lady Bird Johnson and received a lovely personal letter from her encouraging me to go ahead with my ideas about highway beautification. But as I have said, being a judge really prevented me from getting publicly involved in such a project. Lady Bird Johnson is the person responsible for the planting of millions of daffodils on the banks of the Potomac and for many other beautification projects in the City of Washington, DC and in other parts of the US.

The Thomas A Beckett Forest

In 1998, I received one of the greatest honours of my life. A forest was named after me in the Dundas Valley. Previously the Authority had named a trail after me (see cover photo) but it had to be closed due to environmental damage. In 1998, the forest was largely a lovely meadow but the idea was people would be able to plant trees and shrubs as memorials to loved ones and indeed it is already becoming a substantial forest. The official opening of the forest was attended by many local dignitaries, including the Honourable John Munro, and many friends and members of my family. The event was covered by Mary Nolan of the Hamilton Spectator, whose article appeared the next day. Here is a quotation from her article:

> "Beckett is credited with the vision which led to the HRCA's major land acquisition program, including the 1,200 hectares that make up the Dundas Valley Conservation Area. The silver-tongued Beckett used tenacity, persistence and a passionate belief in conservation to get things done - or undone, as was the case with a four-lane expressway planned by the province under former Premier John Robarts.
>
> "It is widely acknowledged that Beckett single-handedly put a stop to the highway project which would have run through the Dundas Valley from Peters Corners to Mohawk Road."

Unveiling of the Thomas A. Beckett Forest plaque

Thomas A. Beckett Forest

This forest is dedicated to the Honourable Thomas A. Beckett, Q.C.

A lifelong conservationist and advocate for the environment, Justice Beckett was instrumental in founding the Spencer Creek Conservation Authority in 1958, serving as Chairman from 1964 to 1966. The Conservation Authority was expanded in 1966 to form the Hamilton Region Conservation Authority, and he continued to serve as Chairman until 1971. Many of the area's major conservation projects were undertaken during his term, most notably the Dundas Valley Conservation Area. With more than 1,200 hectares (3,000 acres) of protected waterfalls, ravines, forest and vistas, the Dundas Valley is one of the most significant natural areas along the world-famous Niagara Escarpment.

In addition to the Valley, Beckett's vigorous and determined leadership set the pace for other major land acquisitions in the watershed, including Conservation Areas located at Valens, Beverly Swamp, Crooks' Hollow, Christie Lake, Tews Falls, Copetown Bog, Tiffany Falls, Mount Albion, Borer's Falls, Devil's Punch Bowl and Fifty Point. A total of 1,538 ha. (3,800 acres) of environmentally significant lands were taken into public trust during his 13 years of service with the Authority.

In recognition of his many conservation achievements, the Hamilton Conservation Foundation established the Thomas A. Beckett Living Forest in 1998.

Another recognition I am very proud of is being inducted into the Hamilton Gallery of Distinction in 1999. The purpose of this award is to recognize and celebrate Hamilton's most distinguished citizens, both past and present. This was not an award for what I was doing as a judge but was certainly an award grounded in the various public contributions I had made in the Hamilton area over the years, not the least of which, of course, was the Conservation Authority. I was greatly honoured to receive this distinguished award.

The Hamilton Conservation Authority 60 Years On

Throughout my time with the Authority it was always my philosophy that we must acquire as much conservation land as possible and as quickly as possible, because I believed we were in a race with urban sprawl and development. The actual development of the lands could wait — acquisition could not. I believe this philosophical principle continued to guide the Authority long after I left.

When I left in 1973, conservation areas totalled about 6,800 acres (2738 ha), consisting of land holdings in the Dundas Valley, Valens, Spencer Gorge, Borer's Falls, Beverly Swamp, Copetown Bog, Albion Falls, Tiffany Falls, Devil's Punchbowl, Crook's Hollow, Christie Lake and Fifty Point.

Today the Hamilton Conservation Authority owns nearly 11,000 acres (nearly 4,400 ha.). It has been a continued policy of the Authority to acquire land. Of course, these are different times: early on, land prices were cheaper and the Government of Ontario provided very generous subsidies towards the purchase of such lands. However, as mentioned earlier, in 1995, the Mike Harris government dropped government assistance to Conservation Authorities from 50% to almost nothing and so it remains. However, through the use of a variety of fundraising methods, they have survived. I am not thrilled about having to charge people to access any conservation land because I always thought they should be available and free to the public, but I do understand the need to raise the funds.

With over 11,000 acres within the Authority's jurisdiction today, it did not occur to me that more public open space might still be acquired. However, as I am writing this, a massive land preservation project comprising of more than 9,000 acres has been identified and is well underway in the Hamilton-Burlington area. It is called the Cootes to Escarpment EcoPark System and is a remarkable collaboration of several agencies in the region, including the Royal Botanical Gardens, the Hamilton Conservation Authority, Conservation Halton, the cities of Burlington and Hamilton, Halton Region and McMaster University. The project is a combination of land acquisition and private stewardship and I am proud of the significant contribution made by the Authority in the planning of this project and the acquisition of several key land holdings.

These thousands of acres of open space, conservation areas and hiking trails all contribute to making Hamilton one of the most liveable cities in Canada. Furthermore, Hamilton has a highly respected university, an extensive health care system which is its leading employer, a vibrant arts community and a burgeoning reputation as a great restaurant destination. All in all, Hamilton is just a great place in which to live and work!

I don't know what other projects the Authority might undertake but I think one of its main functions will be not to just maintain the lands that have been acquired, but to protect them from persons, corporations or even governments, that might have other ideas for their use. The Conservation Authority must be vigilant about who is making donations. You can be sure that any developer who makes a donation to the Authority is not doing it because of a love for conservation and open spaces. You know that when the Nature Conservancy makes a donation you can feel safe. But when a developer or a construction company makes a large donation, look out. I beseech the Authority to keep its eyes on the donor board.

And it's not just developers you have to be careful about. It could be government agencies such as, for example, the Ontario Ministry of Transportation. To my knowledge, after John Robarts quietly killed the Dundas By-Pass, the Ontario Government never officially came out and said that the proposal was dead forever. Although it is highly unlikely, it is always possible that somebody at Queens Park might decide one day that a highway through the valley or through some other environmentally sensitive area is a good idea.

As I have said many times, there is no such thing as too much open space in and around our cities. Have you ever heard of a city anywhere in the world that complains it has too much parkland?

Bribery and Undue influence

I suspect that bribery and dishonesty at the local level of municipal government is very rare. It's more a case of politicians being innocently and unwittingly influenced, particularly by developers. There is nothing illegal about that but it doesn't make it right. I served on the Ancaster Council for seven years, two as a councillor, and five as the Deputy Reeve (mayor). During that time, I did experience one bribery attempt. In the telling of this story I will not use the real names of the persons involved for obvious reasons.

One night, I went to a Council meeting in Ancaster and I pulled into the parking area at the same time as a developer, who was there to meet with the Council. The developer, who I will call Bob, was getting out of his beautiful new Cadillac as I was exiting my old Chevy, and I quipped, "I must be in the wrong business," to which he replied "Do you want one?" I remember being hit with a shot of adrenaline. Was that what I thought it was? We walked into the Council meeting and I must say that those words were ringing in my ears throughout the rest of the evening. I felt very disturbed and angry and as a result I was less than polite during the developer's presentation. I remember going home and telling my wife about what happened and how upset I was. There was nothing I could do about it because I had no evidence of the conversation.

However, the next morning when I arrived at my office I received a telephone call from the developer's lawyer, who was in fact a friend of mine. After the usual greetings he said to me "Tom, that offer you got last night... that was for real". I remember feeling shocked that a friend who knew me so well would make a clear bribery attempt on me. I said to him had I known that he was going to make this phone call to me I would have had the police listening in. And indeed, I would have. He put himself at risk not only for being disbarred but for going to jail. That was the only time I experienced an actual bribery attempt and I can tell you it was a horrible experience. Then I discovered was it was really not necessary for developers to bribe local politicians and officials. They had a better method which was legal and probably less costly.

When I was elected Deputy Reeve I therefore became a member of the Wentworth County Council. I discovered that the Hamilton Homebuilders Association (the developers) put on a banquet each year at the Burlington Golf and Country Club to which all of the members of the Wentworth County and Hamilton City Councils were invited. The first year I was on Council, I made a speech to the other members, saying that we had no business attending a banquet put on by the developers and that we should not attend. Not one other member on the Council supported my position. None of them could see anything wrong with accepting a freebie from the developers. This had been going on for some years and none of them had any intention of giving up on this perk. During the five years I served on the Wentworth County Council I continued to make my annual speech. No one ever supported my position and they all continued to attend this banquet.

I do not know whether the banquet tradition carried on after I left Council, but I do know that a secret committee was formed with representatives from the developers and City officials and politicians. This committee was not open to the public. It had agendas and kept minutes and held private meetings in City Hall. Its existence was kept secret from the public and officials continued to deny its existence. Part of the reason I mention this story is that I discovered a few years ago that the then General Manager of the Conservation Authority was a regular attendee at the meetings. When that was revealed, the then Chairman of the Authority, who was apparently unaware of this committee, stopped this practice.

It must be remembered that conservation authorities and developers have conflicting interests and interactions between the two must always be kept at arm's length and in the public eye. Developers will always look for "legitimate" ways to influence public bodies and the Authority must always remain vigilant of this vulnerability. For-profit corporations exist for only one purpose and that purpose is perfectly legitimate; that is to say, to make a profit. I used to say that if the Steel Company of Canada could make a better profit for their shareholders by churning out butter instead of steel, they would churn out butter.

There is nothing wrong with corporations making a profit for their shareholders. We want them to. As part of doing business in the community, many corporations are able to convince the municipalities in which they operate that they are "good corporate citizens" and make donations to local charities and have officers serve on various boards and commissions, etc. There's nothing wrong with that either. What is wrong is the failure of the people in the community to recognize that corporations are not humans, they don't have souls and are not citizens. They are not public benefactors. They are only legal devices created to allow shareholders to make a profit while limiting their liability. Nothing wrong with that.

On the other hand, public corporations serve the interests of the public. Private for profit corporations serve only the interest of their shareholders and so it should be. What I'm suggesting is that we should always be aware of that. A current example is Hydro One. Hydro One used to exist as a public corporation for the benefit of the people of Ontario. Now that it is privatized, Hydro One only benefits its shareholders, despite what the government may try to tell you about how the public is still protected under this privatization. The fact remains that it is a shareholder corporation whose purpose is to maximize profit for its shareholders, whoever they may be. In the long run, it is difficult to see how this could be in the interest of the public.

And finally...

With my birthday on December 23, 2000 came mandatory retirement from my position as a judge of the Superior Court of Ontario. Fortunately, Meralee was also able to take retirement at the same time from her position as a senior policy advisor with the Ministry of Labour for the Province of Ontario. We have been fortunate to have travelled extensively during the ensuing years, not only to many regions in Canada and throughout the United States, including Alaska, but to England and Wales, France, Spain, Switzerland, Italy, Mexico, and New Zealand. We spend our summers at our beautiful second home on Lake of Bays in Muskoka and for many years wintered in Costa Rica, and more recently in Florida. After we retired, Meralee and I decided we needed to escape the cold Canadian winters and so we decided one winter to rent a house on the beach at a small resort on Playa Ocotal on the North Pacific coast of Costa Rica. We loved it so much that we returned there every winter for 14 years. However, after so many years we were looking for something different and at the urging of my kids, we decided to try Longboat Key on the Florida Gulf Coast where two of them holiday in the winter months. Much to our surprise we really enjoyed vacationing there and have been doing so for a couple of winters now.

I often sit and ponder the future of the human race on this globe. In the long run, I expect it will become extinct just as most other living species on earth have come and gone over time. I am however much more concerned about the short run, that is to say the next hundred years or so.

Climate change caused by humans is fully upon us. The sea levels are rising steadily and swiftly and mankind will have to live with the consequences of this phenomenon. World governments have tried to address this issue with the Paris Climate Accord, for example. Our own government has attempted to address the issue with ways and means of reducing carbon omissions, such as a carbon tax or cap and trade or whatever. But at the same time our government has spent billions of dollars in order to ensure that the Kinder Morgan pipeline is built from the Tar Sands to the Pacific to send oil to be burned in other parts of the globe. What difference does it make whether it is burned in Canada or in China? The emissions all contribute to the same world atmosphere and that seems hypocritical to me. If we were really serious about global warming, we would've found a way to keep Alberta's oil in the ground.

The world of scientific knowledge has reached the point where we can probably solve most of the world's problems of hunger, disease and overpopulation, but having the knowledge to do such things does not mean they will happen. As long as the world is dominated by greed and avarice, ignorance, tribalism, prejudice and religious strife, it is unlikely that knowledge and science will be able to stave off any disastrous results for mankind.

As I reach the end of my path I can look back over my life with some degree of satisfaction and accomplishment. Perhaps my greatest public accomplishment was in the field of conservation and more particularly the work that I did with the Hamilton Conservation Authority. I look with pride at conservation areas such as Valens, Christie, Tews Falls, Fifty Point, Albion Falls, Copetown Bog, Dundas Valley and the Beverly Swamp. Some of these areas would have become conservation areas without my participation, but I believe that I played a pivotal role at the right time; a catalyst you might say. I think I can say with confidence, it was my leadership in leading the public fight against the province's proposal to build a major expressway through the Dundas Valley that resulted in the province abandoning the project.

It's been over 18 years since my retirement from the Bench and I must confess I no longer have the energy to participate in public affairs. Even if I had the desire to get involved, I am content with my retirement years. That is not to say however, that I do not keep my eye on current local affairs, particularly in the area of conservation. I do worry a little bit about the future for the Conservation Authority. I worry about its struggle for money and wonder whether someday the Thomas A. Beckett Forest will go up for sale to some high bidder.

I had a reasonably successful 34 years practicing law earning enough to give my family a good life of travel, cottaging and skiing. I spent 17 years on the Bench, first as a District Court Judge and then as a Judge of the Superior Court. However, my most successful achievement in life has been has been my family. I have three loving children I am close to both physically and emotionally. I have ten grandchildren and five great grandchildren and one more in production. I have a truly wonderful wife and companion, Meralee, who has been at my side for more than 37 years. And it was Meralee who brought three fine stepsons into our marriage. Without her I could not function.

Now my only wish is that when I finally take that last step on what has been a long and interesting path, and leave this life, it will not have been caused by anything too serious.

Tom with his children: Mary-Jo Land, John Beckett and Elizabeth Plashkes.

Tom and the antique canoe he re-finished

About the author

Tom and Meralee Beckett, Lake of Bays, Ontario

Thomas A. Beckett was a lawyer, a judge and a renowned environmentalist and conservationist from the Hamilton Ontario area. He was the first Vice-Chair and then first Chair of the Spencer Creek Conservation Authority and then first Chair of the Hamilton Conservation Authority. During his tenure, the Authority acquired a substantial proportion of the current conservation lands, preserving green space and providing generations to come with access to the magnificent complexity of flora, fauna and geology of the region. Tom's life has been dedicated to his family, his community and the health — locally and globally - of this glorious planet. He lives with his wife, Meralee, in Dundas, Ontario.